INVEST LIKE A WALL STREET ANALYST

mark ettimer

TABLE OF CONTENTS

INTRODUCTION

nvesting in the stock market is a proven way to become wealthy in the United States, but being an individual investor is hard. In order to beat the market and generate above average profits, an investor must have a more informed opinion of a stock than all the other investors who set the price through their trading activity. How is an average retiree, dentist, or hairstylist supposed to compete with the armies of professional analysts working day and night on Wall Street to analyze, value, and invest in stocks? The goal of this book is to teach individual investors like yourself how to evaluate and choose stocks like a professional equity research analyst. It is not a get-rich-quick strategy; it will take effort and persistence, but the potential rewards make it worthwhile. By evaluating stocks like a professional using the strategies laid out in this book, I believe it is possible to get all the benefits of an actively managed stock portfolio while saving considerable money on expensive mutual fund and other money management fees. All that is required for anyone to use the strategies in this book is middle school math, basic computer literacy, common sense, and some effort.

Investing can be interesting and even fun, but it should not be confused with entertainment. The serious business of choosing stocks requires dedicated effort over a long period of time. But it does not have to be (and should not be) a full time job for the individual investor. By focusing on the analysis that adds the most value, you can manage your portfolio of stocks like a professional while working full time or enjoying retirement.

INVEST LIKE A WALL STREET ANALYST

Understanding the competition is key to winning in any business, and investing is no different. This book will explain the business of equity research on Wall Street, to help individuals understand how professionals operate and how to gain an edge. Once that is firmly understood, we will start exploring how to adapt those activities to the requirements and abilities of an individual investor.

This book will explain the most common strategies and techniques for choosing stocks utilized by Wall Street equity research analysts, but each reader may choose to adopt some or all of them based on their personal style and preference. What works well for some investors does not necessarily work for others. But some of the fundamentals, such as careful reading of a company's financial disclosures, are a requirement for anyone to successfully invest in stocks. Changes in expectations about future earnings and cash flow or prevailing valuation metrics can result in outsized investment opportunities. Analysts must have a good understanding of these fundamentals to be able to spot those opportunities and earn above average profits.

An avid reader could fill a library with volumes about the topics covered in this book like financial statement analysis, financial modeling, and portfolio management. This book will be thorough enough for serious amateurs to begin investing on their own, and may even inspire further research into some of these topics.

The book will help readers understand how to read an equity research report and extract as much valuable information as possible. For the uninitiated, it can be hard to know where to start or how to interpret a Wall Street research report. But once you have gained a good understanding of the business of equity research, analyst reports can be an invaluable aid to your investment activities.

Through detailed explanations of analytical techniques and concrete examples, the reader will gain an understanding of how a professional analyst synthesizes information to make good stock picks and learn how to implement those techniques for him or herself. But simply making good stock picks isn't enough to achieve your financial goals- the book will also walk the reader through strategies for trading and managing a portfolio in order to maximize financial outcomes. While beating the market in a given year is never a guarantee, managing your portfolio efficiently to avoid fees and common investing mistakes is almost certain to improve financial performance and gives you a head start over professionally managed mutual funds.

The ultimate goal of any investing book is to help the reader maximize their investment returns so they can achieve their financial goals, and this is no exception. Gaining insight into professional ways to manage a portfolio of stocks is one of the best ways to improve returns by reducing fee drag and creating the potential for above-market returns.

CHAPTER ONE

WHAT AN EQUITY RESEARCH ANALYST DOES

There are many misconceptions about how equity research analysts at large brokerages like Bank of America, JP Morgan, and Goldman Sachs operate. To understand the business of equity research, you must first understand how these firms' research departments make money.

Equity research analysts employed by Wall Street brokers attempt to provide valuable information to their clients, primarily large institutional investors like mutual funds, hedge funds, sovereign wealth funds, and others who invest in the stock market. In the US, clients do not pay directly for access to research. Instead, they reward the firm by directing their trading commissions to the broker's trading desk. Having a well-known research analyst covering a given sector can also help a broker win equity underwriting business from corporate clients, who hope to have their stocks covered by prestigious analysts who will generate interest in their company. It is important to understand that Wall Street analysts are not directly compensated for the performance of their stock picks, nor do they sell their services directly to their clients. They operate in something of an informal barter economy, where research analysts generate goodwill that results in a broader business relationship as a fee- or commission-paying client of the firm. These indirect payments for research are known in the industry as "soft dollars".

In addition to financial compensation, top equity research analysts are recognized by a widely read industry publication called Institutional Investor magazine each year. Top analysts are named to Institutional Investor's All-America Research team based on a survey of research clients. This recognition is highly coveted among Wall Street analysts.

The intended audience of a Wall Street equity research analyst is made up of investment professionals. Research analysts employed by brokers are considered "sell side" analysts, because they are using research to sell the firm's financial services. The clients of these analysts are considered "buy side" analysts, because they are the ones making the decision to buy stocks. Buy side analysts gain valuable information and insight from sell side analysts, but they always do their own homework before buying a stock.

What services do sell side analysts provide that are of value to their clients? Analysts are assigned to cover a particular industry sector and are expected to be experts on their coverage universe. Analysts convey their expertise and information they gather about stocks to clients in a variety of ways. Analysts publish research reports that contain a written digest and analysis of information about the company and its markets. In addition, analysts may have phone calls or in-person meetings with clients to discuss their thoughts on a company. Research analysts also can arrange meetings between company management teams and investors, referred to as "corporate access", either in a conference or a one-on-one setting.

Written research reports are typically the most visible aspect of a research analyst's work. An analyst starts coverage of a stock with an "initiating coverage" report. This report is typically a highly detailed writeup of the company's business, markets, competitive environment, and financial condition. Information from this report is gathered from a variety of sources: company financial reports and other disclosures, government statistics, industry association publications, news reports, conversations with management, and other sources. The analyst will launch an initial buy, sell, or hold recommendation and a price target for the stock. In connection with this, the analyst will build a financial projection model. On an ongoing basis, the analyst issues update reports in response to quarterly earnings, significant news about the company, industry developments, or new trading ideas. The analyst may also write research reports about the industry or other thematic research pieces about trends affecting the business.

The role of the analyst has changed over time in response to market forces and regulation. Prior to the tech bubble of 2000-2001, analysts often gave inflated positive recommendations in order to please corporate clients and win business underwriting new initial public offerings. In response to that, New York State Attorney General Elliot Spitzer led a regulatory effort that resulted in the Global Analyst Research Settlements in 2003. In addition to harsh monetary penalties, brokers agreed as part of these settlements to make significant changes to their businesses to manage conflicts of interest and improve the quality and independence of equity research. Brokers were required to separate equity research from investment banking businesses, including total separation of analyst coverage responsibilities and compensation to prevent the type of conflict of interest that resulted in inflated buy recommendations prior to the settlement. Other changes such as enhanced disclosures and information firewalls between research and other parts of the firm were implemented as well. Research analysts at underwriting banks do still play a role in the initial public offering process for issuance of new stock, but it is strictly managed by internal compliance personnel to ensure their role is independent and limited to "investor education", which by rule cannot communicate an investment opinion. An investment opinion cannot be communicated until coverage is formally initiated following a quiet period after the IPO.

In 2000, the Securities and Exchange Commission passed a rule called Regulation Full Disclosure, or "Reg FD", to prevent material information being passed from companies to investors on a selective basis. Since the implementation of Reg FD, any material information that is disclosed to one investor or analyst must be disclosed to all investors simultaneously to prevent any unfair advantages for favored investors. For analysts who often deal directly with company management, Reg FD is an important rule that limits the advantages that used to benefit professional analysts over individuals.

In 2018, European regulators introduced Markets in Financial Instruments Directive II, or "MiFID II", an expansive regulatory framework promoting transparency in financial markets that affected research among many other aspects of the industry. Most notably for research analysts, MiFID II required research to be "unbundled", that is, to be sold separately rather than given away in exchange for "soft dollar" brokerage commissions and other paid financial services as it typically had been. This regulation marked a major change in the business of equity research for analysts operating in the European Union.

Aside from regulatory pressure, equity research analysts have also been impacted by market trends. Over the last two decades, investors have increasingly invested in the stock market through so-called "passive" investments such as index funds and exchange traded funds. Passive investments allocate money to stocks based on an index benchmark, such as the S&P 500, and do not seek to improve returns by actively choosing stocks that will outperform. Passive investments have become extremely popular as a way to avoid expensive money management fees. Investment research firm Morningstar reported that in mid-2019, assets allocated to passive stock market investments surpassed actively managed investments for the first time. This has drained assets from institutional investors that are clients of equity research analysts and therefore shrunk the market opportunity for equity research. As a result, research coverage has suffered. Many smaller brokerages have closed their research departments altogether.

Equity research is an extremely competitive business. The most successful equity research analysts bring together a range of skills. They pay great attention to detail and have the ability to multitask, especially after the end of a quarter when many companies are reporting updated financial results around the same time. Good research analysts know how to ask the right questions and be persistent in finding answers. A good analyst has a reputation for being knowledgeable, but isn't afraid to "look stupid" if it means asking a basic question that needs to be asked. Analysts are good inductive reasoners, meaning they are able to pull together pieces of seemingly unrelated information to form a coherent, actionable conclusion. They obviously must be good writers, since much of their work product is contained in written research reports. In addition to the technical finance and accounting skills that are basic requirements of working in financial services, they have good people skills. They can communicate an investment idea and persuade clients to put their money behind it. At the end of the day, the best analysts are great storytellers. The job of an analyst is to take bits of information and weave them together into a narrative that explains where a company is today, where it is going, and what that means for its investors, and to do so in a concise and compelling way.

CHAPTER TWO

PICK A SECTOR

You are ready to start choosing stocks like a professional equity research analyst. The first step is to choose an industry to cover. Forming a well-thought out, professional opinion on the entire universe of publicly traded companies is an impossible task even for a full time professional. Even knowing where to begin looking for opportunities within that set would be difficult. A professional research analyst is assigned to cover a particular industry sector, and within that subset of companies he or she is able to develop a base of knowledge to thoughtfully evaluate a group of stocks and react quickly to news. Similarly, individual investors should focus their efforts on a relatively small group of related stocks and become an expert on that sector.

Choose an industry that is interesting to you, that you can understand, and that you can trade. This may be an industry with which you have firsthand experience: a medical doctor or pharmaceutical sales rep might focus on pharmaceutical stocks. An avid shopper might choose fashion, retail, or restaurants. A data center manager might choose networking hardware stocks. Alternatively, you may choose an industry with a strong local presence, such as the oil & gas industry for an investor who lives in Texas. Another option is to choose an industry based on a theme about which you are interested and knowledgeable. For example, a technophile may choose to follow internet or semiconductor stocks. A geopolitics or news junkie may want to follow the energy sector. If an investor is interested in the macroeconomy, a highly cyclical sector like the staffing industry may present opportunities.

Make sure whatever sector you choose is one that you can understand and one that has good investment prospects. Do not choose a sector like insurance if you do not understand the products, how the companies make money, or factors that drive profitability like interest rates. Also avoid sectors that are too small to have many investable opportunities. Your sector should be defined broadly enough to include several investable stocks, and should have good enough growth prospects to make those stocks interesting. If you choose corporate records management as your sector, you will really only have one publicly-traded investment opportunity- Iron Mountain. It would be more productive to define your coverage universe more broadly to include other stocks, such as business services stocks or data center stocks in this case. Avoid choosing a sector simply because its stocks have performed well recently. Recent performance is never guaranteed to continue, and if performance deteriorates and you have not selected the sector based on other good criteria, you may not have the interest or knowledge to maintain your coverage.

Possible sector choices are listed below, broken down by MSCI's Global Industry Classification Standard (GICS)®. Depending on the depth and diversity of each category, you may be able to narrow down your selection even further beyond these categories to more niche sub-sectors if that is more interesting or practical for you.

GICS Sectors

Sector	Subsectors
Energy	
Materials	
Industrials	Capital Goods
	Commercial & Professional Services
	Transportation
Consumer Discretionary	Autos
	Consumer Durables & Apparel
	Consumer Services
	Retailing
Consumer Staples	Food & Staples Retailing
	Food, Beverage & Tobacco
	Household & Personal Products
Healthcare	Healthcare Equipment & Services
	Pharmaceuticals, Biotechnology & Life Sciences
Financials	Banks
	Diversified Financials
	Insurance
Information Technology	Software & Services
	Technology, Hardware & Equipment
	Semiconductors & Semiconductor Equipment
Communications Services	Telecommunication Services
	Media & Entertainment
Utilities	
Real Estate	

Once you have selected a sector that meets your criteria, you must begin to identify sources of information. An analyst must keep tabs on general business and economic news as well as industry specific information. General news sources could include local or national news outlets, such as the Wall Street

Journal, CNN, CNBC, or Bloomberg Businessweek. Major economic data releases such as GDP, unemployment, inflation, and Federal Reserve announcements should also be followed with an eye toward how developments might affect your sector. Industry information sources could include government data, relevant industry association publications, academic research, or even your own primary research, among others. Some of the more commonly used data sources are organized in the table below; this is not an exhaustive list by any means, but could be a good starting point if you are researching a new industry.

MARK ETTIMER

Source	Data Sets	Sample Relevant Industries
Bureau of Economic Analysis	Gross Domestic Product (GDP)	all
www.bea.gov	Personal Income	all
	International Trade	all
Bureau of Labor Statistics	Employment	all
www.bls.gov	Consumer Price Index	all
	Producer Price Index	all
Census Bureau	Retail Sales	All, Consumer
www.census.gov	Construction Spending	Real Estate, Industrial
	Manufacturers' Shipments, Inventories, & Orders	Industrial
	New Residential Home Sales	Real Estate, Financial, Utilities
Centers for Medicare & Medicaid Services	Medicare Drug Spending	Healthcare
www.cms.gov	Medicare Provider Utilization & Payment Data	Healthcare
Congressional Budget Office	Government Budget Data & Projections	Aerospace & Defense
www.cbo.gov		
Energy Information Administration	Crude Oil Inventories	Energy
www.eia.gov	Energy Outlook Reports	All, Energy
	Wholesale Electricity Market Data	Utilities
Federal Energy Regulatory Commission	Power Market Assessments	Utilities
www.ferc.gov		
Federal Reserve	Consumer Credit	Financial, Consumer, Real Estate
www.federalreserve.gov	Loan Officer Surveys	Financial, Consumer, Real Estate
	Industrial Production	Industrial
	Interest Rates	All, Financial, Consumer, Real Estate
Food and Drug Administration	Clinical Trial Data	Healthcare
www.fda.gov		
IHS Markit	PMI	Industrial
www.markiteconomics.com		
University of Michigan	Consumer Confidence Index	All, Consumer Durable, Consumer Discretionary
www.sca.isr.umich.edu		

INVEST LIKE A WALL STREET ANALYST

The Federal Reserve Bank of St. Louis offers a very helpful tool called Federal Reserve Economic Data or FRED® (http://fred.stlouisfed.org). FRED is a charting tool that pulls economic data from a variety of sources into one convenient place. The National Bureau of Economic Research (http://www.nber.org) also helpfully aggregates a lot of economic data releases into one place. Many financial websites offer economic calendars that helps keep track of upcoming data releases, which can help analysts stay on top of the latest data as it is released.

Once you have identified the relevant sources of information, an analyst must spend time to analyze historical data and its impact on the stocks that will be covered. Look for connections between data points and stock market performance. Try to learn when important data is typically released in order to keep up with the latest developments and update your view on the sector if necessary.

As an example, some industry information relevant to the US staffing sector is compiled below. The staffing sector includes companies that employ temporary workers who provide services of all kinds to companies in the United States. Roughly one out of every 50 workers in the United States currently is a temp, so it is a large, important industry with several publicly-traded companies, and one about which many people have firsthand knowledge. Staffing is a subset of the industrial / commercial and professional services sector. The Bureau of Labor Statistics, a division of the US Department of Labor, provides a wealth of information that is relevant to the overall economy and the staffing industry specifically, including data on temporary worker employment and pricing. Looking at the historical data, it is apparent that the staffing industry is highly cyclical (note that the shaded areas indicate economic recessions):

Total Temporary Help Employment (thousands)

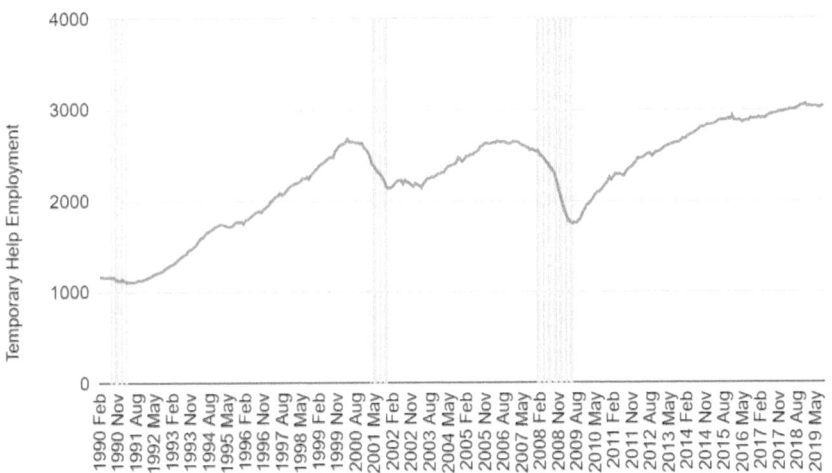

It is commonly believed that temporary staffing is counter-cyclical, that is, that staffing companies perform better in a weak economy and vice versa. This is often assumed because temporary workers may be less expensive, and companies are less likely to make permanent hires during a recession. That seems like a logical guess, however, an analysis of the data shows that it is totally wrong! By looking at the percentage of US workers that are employed on a temporary basis (the "Temporary Worker Penetration Rate"), it can clearly be seen that temporary workers are cut further and faster in a downturn than permanent workers, and furthermore, temporary employment rebounds faster and continues to grow as fast or faster than overall employment throughout the expansion cycle. Professional analysts do not just make assumptions, they look at the data!

Temporary Worker Penetration Rate

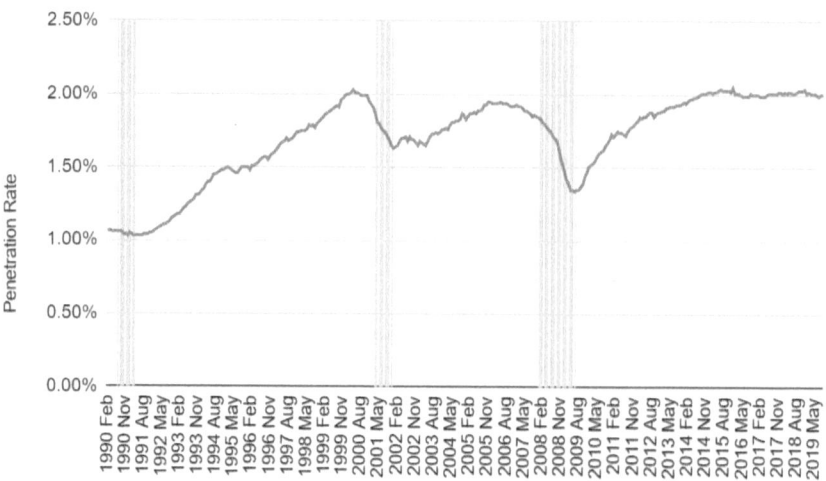

The Bureau of Labor Statistics also provides information on the cost of temporary workers in the Producer Price Index, or "PPI". Does a rising price of temporary labor allow staffing companies to improve profitability by raising prices, or does it hurt profitability due to rising costs? A comparison of PPI data to EBITDA margins (earnings before interest, taxes, depreciation, and amortization, an important measure of profitability of a company's operations) at Robert Half International Inc. (RHI), a large US staffing firm, shows that rising prices are actually good for profit margins, while falling prices are correlated with decreased profitability.

Change in Staffing PPI and RHI EBITDA Margin

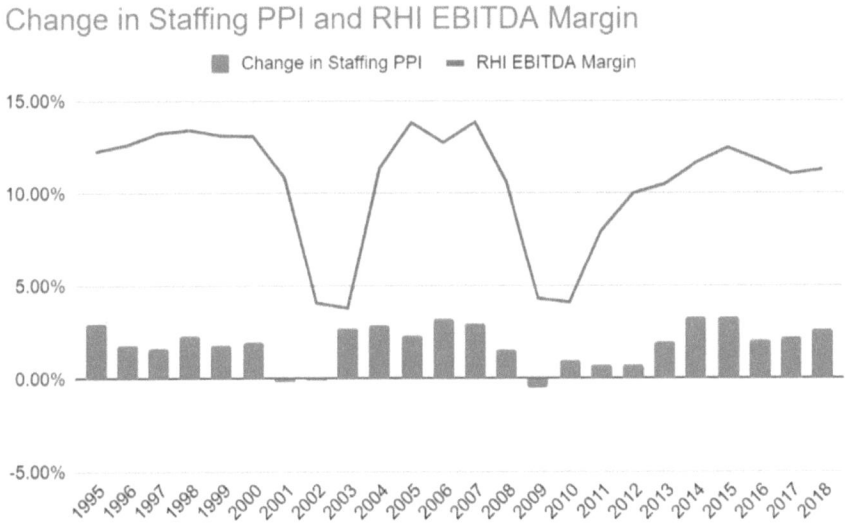

This knowledge will be of major importance to anyone thinking about the outlook for stocks of staffing companies. Another important source of information from the government for this industry is the Federal Reserve Beige Book, a document published eight times per year that includes surveys of the staffing industry. Industry associations can also be an extremely valuable source of information. For staffers, the American Staffing Association publishes important industry news, data, and surveys, including the ASA Staffing Index, which can give important updates on the state of the industry that are more frequent than the quarterly financial reports issued by publicly traded companies.

Staffing Jobs Hold Steady in October

SHARE: October 22, 2019

ASA Staffing Index Monthly Report, October 2019

Staffing jobs for the week of Oct. 7–13 changed little from the prior week (-0.05%), remaining at a value of 97 for five consecutive weeks, according to the ASA Staffing Index. Survey respondents cited school breaks and holidays as factors that limited growth. Staffing employment was 4.9% lower than the same week last year, but still on trend with levels seen in prior recent years.

The ASA Staffing Index four-week moving average held at a rounded value of 97. Staffing jobs for the four weeks ending Oct. 13 were down 5.4% from 2018, remaining below last year's record highs.

This week, containing the 12th day of the month, will be used in the October monthly employment situation report that will be issued by the U.S. Bureau of Labor Statistics on Nov. 1.

The ASA Staffing Index is reported nine days after each workweek, making it a near real-time measure of staffing employment trends. ASA research shows that staffing employment has historically been a coincident economic indicator.

For more information, visit *americanstaffing.net/index*. Or follow ASA research on Twitter.

# # #

Some industry associations may require paid membership or subscriptions to access information. Depending on your situation and the sector you have chosen, you may wish to pay for this type of information, or you may feel it is not necessary.

It is important to scour any news that could be relevant to your companies. Google.com/alerts allows analysts to set up news alerts tied to particular keywords, such as the name of a company or economic indicator. These alerts can be extremely helpful for staying informed about your sector. You may wish to set up a separate email account specifically for these types of emails to track them efficiently without interfering with your personal correspondence.

In addition to information that is widely available on the web, you may also have the opportunity to develop some personal networks in the industry. Professional equity research analysts rely on their personal networks to get differentiated market intelligence that is valuable to their clients. For example, if you get to know the owners of a few small local staffing firm, they may be able to provide you with some interesting market intelligence or an informed opinion on the macroeconomic environment.

If you are not already familiar with the sources of information that are available in your industry, finding them can be as simple as using an internet search engine. You may also see certain data sources mentioned in news stories about your companies or industries, or they may even be mentioned by the companies themselves in investor presentations or other disclosures. Pay attention to what information sources are referenced in the news and financial media and by companies, and start following some of them directly on your own.

Once you have gathered all the information you are able to about your industry, it is time to formulate a view on secular trends that will affect your stocks. These could include changes in demographics, technology, regulation, or consumer preferences that will shape the long-term outlook for stocks in your sector. Identify opportunities and risks that these trends create. To again use the example of staffing stocks, the data suggest a long term trend toward use of temporary workers by companies who value flexibility in the wake of the deep recession in 2007-2009. Technology has made "gig work" easier- there is no shortage of apps and websites connecting companies to workers for short term assignments, and this has led to increased interest in temporary work and other alternative work arrangements by many people. A risky development is that these trends have naturally attracted the attention of regulators and labor unions, who are increasingly eager to exert their influence over this growing segment of the US labor market in ways that could negatively affect growth and profitability for staffing companies.

In addition to secular trends, the analyst should look for cyclical patterns in the historical data. The business cycle, i.e. the growth and contraction of the economy over time (as measured by gross domestic product, or "GDP") will be important to most stocks, but it is important to figure out what indicators are most relevant to your sector. As can be seen in the charts above, staffing is a very pro-cyclical sector and tends to lead the broader economy into and out of recessions. As you get started, remember that each sector is different. A pharmaceutical analyst might be more concerned with clinical trial schedules and results published by the Food and Drug Administration than with GDP or other economic data. Figuring out what information is important is an extremely important step and will be different for each industry.

If all of this seems daunting, remember that you do not have to build Rome in one day. Professional analysts develop and refine their knowledge of a sector over a period of years before becoming the lead publishing analyst at their firm. Your base of knowledge and sources of information will grow over time as you continue to cover your sector. You may even wish to cover your sector for a few months or even longer before actually deploying money behind your ideas in order to develop more confidence in your knowledge and abilities.

CHAPTER THREE

INITIATE COVERAGE

N ow that you have a strong understanding of industry issues and trends, you are able to take the next step and begin researching individual companies within your sector. First, you must identify which companies are in your target coverage universe. You may do this by visiting informational websites like Yahoo! Finance (http://finance.yahoo.com) or Google Finance (http://www.google.com/finance) or your broker's website to search for stocks, or you may see companies mentioned in the news. Some publicly traded companies may not be worth your time to cover. They may be too small, be in financial distress, or otherwise be unsuitable for investment. While these companies may be worth tracking casually because they provide interesting information in their investor disclosures that is relevant to other companies you cover, they are not worth your scarce time and attention to cover full time because they do not present an investment opportunity.

It can be dangerous to cover too many companies, because with constraints on your time and attention, you will not be able to develop a truly informed opinion of any one of them. A professional equity research analyst may cover 15 or 20 stocks on average. You may choose to cover more or fewer, depending on your situation. The more homogenous your coverage universe is, the more stocks you can safely cover. For example, real estate investment trust (REIT) analysts tend to have larger coverage universes because REIT stocks tend to be fairly homogenous. Ultimately, you should cover enough stocks to provide a diverse pool of investment options, but not so many that you cannot keep tabs on them all.

Once you have identified which stocks you will cover, it is time to develop a base of knowledge about each company that will enable you to make informed investment decisions about the stock. A good starting point is each company's investor relations web page. A variety of resources will normally be available on the web page including investor presentations, financial disclosures (sometimes referred to as "SEC filings"), earnings call transcripts, news releases, and more. Most companies will provide an option to subscribe to email alerts, which is a good idea (again, it can be useful to create a separate email account specifically for these types of emails).

The company's annual report will be available through the investor relations webpage (and if it is not, annual reports are always filed and available along with any other company filings on the Securities and Exchange Commission's website by visiting http://www.sec.gov/edgar). Reading this document is the single most important step in learning about a new company. It will help you understand the business, recent financial performance, risk factors and accounting policies.

These documents can be several hundred pages long, and there is typically some boilerplate that can be skimmed, but it is impossible to overstate the importance of reading these reports. The annual report is filed with the Securities and Exchange Commission on form 10-K. Every 10-K has the same basic organization, as laid out below:

Item 1: Business

Analysts will typically read this section in detail to understand what the company does and how it is organized. This section also includes a list of risk factors, which are important to understand. Some risk factors will be more generic and others will be more specific to the business. It is important to understand each one. It is also important to note when new risk factors are added to this section, as it is often a sign that the company sees potential challenges ahead. If there are unresolved comments from SEC staff on previous filings, they will be included as well. There typically will be none, and if there are any, they may be a red flag.

Item 2: Properties

Depending on the business this section may or may not be quite long. An asset-intensive business like a manufacturer or real estate company may have a long list of properties. An asset-light company (say, one that provides professional services) will have a shorter list.

Item 3: Legal proceedings

Almost all companies are involved in lawsuits as part of their day to day operations. Most are not material to the stock price, but this section should be read and anything material should be considered when developing an investment thesis. Material legal issues will often be discussed in the risk factors in Item 1 as well.

Item 4: Mine safety disclosures

This section is usually blank (unless of course the company operates mines).

Item 5: Market for the company's stock

This is basic information about the shares and may include some interesting information on share buybacks, though everything in this section is typically available in other places so an experienced analyst shouldn't expect to find much new information here. One thing of interest for a new analyst will be which peers the company chooses to compare itself to. That information can be a good starting point for peer comparisons, but should not necessarily be considered an exhaustive list of comparable companies.

Item 6: Selected financial data

This section includes a few key indicators of financial performance often over a longer historical timeframe than is included in the full financial statements.

Item 7: Management's discussion and analysis of financial results

This section is an explanation of the company's reported financial results, and often includes an overview of key accounting policies. Analysts should read this section in detail, particularly when learning about a new company, but much of the historical information will already be familiar if you have been covering a company for a long time.

Item 8: Financial Statements

This section is where full financial results are reported according to Generally Accepted Accounting Principles (GAAP) along with certain supplemental information.

Notes

After the financial statements are notes, which are important disclosures and additional information that help analysts interpret the financial statements. Notes concerning debt and taxes are typically interesting sources of information that is not found elsewhere. The notes also typically have good information on financial performance by business segment which can be very important to analyze.

Other Information

Certain other required disclosures and signatures by senior management are also included in these filings. These can fill many pages, but are typically of less interest to analysts except in some unusual situations.

ↄↄↄↄↄↄↄↄↄ

From time to time a new company may sell shares to the public for the first time in an initial public offering (IPO). When a company intends to complete an IPO, it will file a prospectus with the SEC on form S-1. This filing contains much of the same information as an annual report, but has additional information on the offering of securities and often has additional information about the business and industry. If a company completed its IPO within the last few years, the S-1 filing can be a very valuable source of information.

Many companies also post an investor presentation on their website. This can be a helpful way to get up to speed on a company and get a quick overview of their financial situation and goals. Keep in mind that these are marketing documents, so they will naturally present things in the most favorable light possible for the company, but they contain valuable information for analysts. Even for experienced analysts, when a new presentation is released, it is interesting to carefully compare to previous versions and note any changes.

After each quarter, companies release their latest financial results and hold a conference call with investors. When looking at a new company for the first time, it can be helpful to reconstruct the last few quarters by reading the earnings press releases, related presentations, and earnings conference call transcripts and comparing them to the stock price history to get a sense for how reported results are impacting the stock price. Transcripts are sometimes available on the company's investor relations website, but they can also be found on financial websites like Seeking Alpha (http://seekingalpha.com) or Motley Fool (http://www.fool.com). As an alternative to reading the transcripts, most companies post audio replays of the conference call on their website. Some analysts believe listening to the recording is better because it provides cues based on management's or analysts' tone of voice while speaking.

At this point you will likely have questions about the business. One of the hardest parts of an analyst's job is figuring out what the right questions to ask are, because that requires deeply understanding the business and what factors might cause the stock price to go up or down. Once you have a good understanding of the business, you can start asking intelligent questions about how the company will generate returns for shareholders and searching for the answers. Most investor relations websites will include contact information for the company's investor relations department. You may reach out to the company with questions directly, but as a small investor, the likelihood you will get a good answer is low. Aside from Reg FD concerns, investor relations departments are typically focused on marketing the company's stock to the largest institutional investors, which alone can be overwhelming. To find answers to some questions, you may have to be creative and entrepreneurial. You may have to go to a store and test the company's products along with its competitors. Ask other shoppers what they think about them and why. Look at online reviews to get a sense of what people are saying. If you are researching a healthcare company, perhaps you may get an expert opinion from a medical doctor you know. It is often surprising how much people are willing to help when you ask questions, even if you don't know them well. And do not stop at researching only the company in question; if you know the company has publicly traded suppliers or customers, try to glean what information you can from their public filings as well. Do whatever you can think of to track down information that could help you make a good investment decision.

Another important aspect of equity analysis is ownership of the stock. A snapshot of who owns the stock is available in the annual Definitive 14A filing, which is available on any company's investor relations website or the SEC's website. There is a natural conflict of interest between the owners (shareholders) and managers of a business. Owners simply want the highest financial returns on their investment. Managers may have other goals, like expanding their personal influence by adding other lines of business, regardless of whether that activity produces good returns on investment. Higher ownership of a company by management may result in better decision making, because every decision affects the management team's wealth as much as investors'. The Definitive 14A will have information on management pay as well, which should be structured to align the interests of management with those of investors. Definitive 14A filings now include results of non-binding "say on pay" votes in which investors are given the opportunity to express satisfaction with management's pay. A strong result in the say on pay vote is a good indication that professional investors view the management team as being well aligned with investors.

With the information available to you, you should start to develop your own analysis of the company's strategy and its financial performance, and in turn start projecting what financial performance will look like in the future and figuring out a fair value for the stock. The next few chapters will cover all of these topics in greater detail.

Based on all the work you have done, develop and write down an investment thesis, that is, an explanation of why you would invest in this company. Try to identify the positive factors that could cause the stock price to go up. Even if you are not bullish on the stock, put yourself in the shoes of someone who is and try to figure out why they are buying. Next, identify the risk factors that could cause that investment thesis to fail. They could be risks facing the entire industry like macroeconomic trends or regulations, or things that are more specific to the company in question like loss of market share or declining profitability. You may identify risks resulting from anything you have learned about the economic environment, competitors, products, customers, costs, or any number of other things. You should develop a balanced and realistic view of the strengths and risks of the business.

Professional analysts sometimes choose not to cover a company because the information flow is inadequate for making an investment decision. It may be because the reporting is confusing or because management refuses to speak to analysts. If you believe a Company's disclosures are confusing or inadequate, you don't necessarily have to beat your head against a wall trying to understand the company. It may be unlikely you will ever be able to develop an informed view of the company anyway. In those situations, you may simply choose to monitor the company for any interesting information they provide about the sector without developing a full investment recommendation or price target. However, if you are able to glean more insight into a difficult situation than other investors, that can be very fertile ground for finding the most attractive investment opportunities.

Initiating coverage of a new company is a big task. There is a lot of reading and a lot of work involved. But once you have done the work, the effort level required to maintain an educated opinion on the stock will usually be much less, though you may need to refresh your view if something fundamental changes in the industry or if the company completes a transformative acquisition or divestiture. In general, you will be able to quickly process new information about the company because a strong foundation is already there. This strong foundation is one of the key advantages of investing like a Wall Street equity research analyst.

CHAPTER FOUR

STRATEGIC ANALYSIS

Knowing how a company operates is only the first step in understanding a business. To make an informed judgment about a company, an analyst needs to have an understanding of its strategy. A successful management team must have a strategy for maintaining and growing the company. There is no one strategy that will work for all companies. Analyzing a strategy for a business requires understanding the company's strengths and weaknesses (internal factors) and its competitive market environment (external factors).

The first step in analyzing a business strategy is looking across an organization and making a determination of the company's strengths and weaknesses. What does a business do well? Is it good product development? Innovation? A brand that is stronger than its peers? More efficient manufacturing operations? A better management team? Once you know a company's strengths, ask how management is utilizing those strengths in the marketplace. For example, a company with a strong brand may use that as an opportunity to grow their retail shelf space, or to add new product line expansions under a familiar brand to generate growth. For public stock investors, it can be hard to make a complete judgment about what a company does well without having access to the company's inner workings, but many of the company's strengths will be evident from the outside. If a company's product is the best in the market, that will come through in market share statistics and customer reviews.

As with most things in life, strategy usually involves tradeoffs. It is probably impossible for any one company to be the best at everything they do. If a company invests in having the most diverse set of products to appeal to the widest array of customers and win the most retail shelf space, it may end up having a cost disadvantage due to the operational complexity of manufacturing that product line. If management of a company that has a very strong business-to-consumer brand announces that they are going to grow rapidly by focusing on business-to-business sales, that may in fact be a growth opportunity, but it may also be an indicator that the company is veering off course. It is important to analyze a company's growth strategy to determine how realistic or how risky it is.

Any analysis of internal factors is incomplete without also comparing a company to its competition. A useful framework for understanding a business' competitive environment is Porter's Five Forces model. Developed by Harvard Business School professor Michael Porter in 1979, this model provides a framework for understanding key factors that influence a business' ability to generate profits. The forces in the model are:

Threat of new entrants

How easy is it for another firm to start competing in this business? It is very easy for anyone to open a new restaurant and start competing in that sector. It is not so easy, however, to start a new electric utility company in your town. The easier it is to enter and compete, the harder it will be for a business to maintain a high level of profitability.

Threat of substitutes

Can your company's product be easily replaced with something else? A drug that is off patent can easily be substituted with a generic drug, but a patented drug cannot be easily substituted. For that reason, you would expect profit margins on generic drugs to be much lower than those of patented drugs, and indeed they are.

Bargaining power of customers

Who are the customers of the business and how much ability do they have to influence pricing? A very concentrated customer base typically has more leverage to negotiate lower pricing. A defense company whose only customer is the US government would likely have a harder time maintaining pricing and profitability than a software company that sells products to individual consumers and businesses all across the country. How easy is it for customers to switch purchases to a competitor? If it is very easy for customers to switch purchases between competitors, it will be easier for them to negotiate better pricing by playing competitors off each other. When switching is difficult or costly, companies can maintain better pricing. A classic example of business with relatively high cost of switching is razors and razorblades. In order to switch razorblade brands, you also need to buy a new razor that is compatible.

Bargaining power of suppliers

Most businesses need to buy raw material or inputs from other companies in order to create the product that they ultimately sell to their customers. A highly concentrated supplier landscape, such as for a specialty chemical that is only manufactured in certain parts of the world, means the business will have a harder time capturing profits than for a business that uses a widely available input, like whole wheat flour. It is important to understand the supply chain for the industry you are analyzing. Labor is an important input and significant cost for many companies. A unionized workforce is likely to have more bargaining power than a non-unionized one. In general, concentrated suppliers of raw materials or labor will lead to a lower level of sustainable profits at a company.

Competitive intensity

Competitive intensity describes the activity of other firms selling competing products or services. How aggressively do firms compete on price? How much differentiation exists between products? The more unique the product, the better a company will be able to maintain its profitability. Not all industries have the same competitive dynamics. Two gas stations across the street from one another might compete ruthlessly on price every day, while two upscale boutiques might both sell handbags on the same block at a premium price and never worry about undercutting each other.

↗↘↗↘↗↘↗↘↗↘↗↘↗

Ideally a business should be able to identify some kind of competitive advantage over other firms in its industry. A competitive advantage is anything that makes it hard for a company to lose its customers to other firms. This advantage can come in many forms. If customers know a company's brand and trust it, they are more likely to purchase the company's product than its peers, and may even be willing to pay more for it. If a company has the most efficient, high tech manufacturing operations, or unique access to raw materials or labor, it may be able to put product on the market at a price point its competitors can't match. Reputation may form a significant competitive advantage. It is an old adage that no one ever got fired for hiring Goldman Sachs to advise on an acquisition, but taking a chance on an unknown adviser might cost a manager his career if things don't go well. Scale can also be an important advantage because in most cases size leads to efficiencies. Walmart is a great example of a company that has used size to its advantage, negotiating better prices with suppliers, optimizing logistics across a huge network of stores, and advertising efficiently to customers nationwide.

Strategy should also take into account the prevailing market environment. Market environments for almost all businesses are constantly changing due to things like demographics, technology, and consumer preferences, which creates opportunities and risks for every company. Managers must make a decision about what lines of business to compete in or avoid. Good management teams are adept at spotting and reacting to opportunities, such as entering new, higher growth markets, or markets where competition is relatively weak. They should also appropriately weigh risk, and seek to position their companies well for difficult times when market trends move against them or competition intensifies. Riskier strategies typically involve more radical change: perhaps entering new product categories or geographic markets where the company has less experience, launching a totally new brand, making significant changes to pricing, or entering a more volatile market where customer tastes change frequently.

While setting the course for a multibillion dollar business can be highly complex, a strong management team should be able to articulate its strategy and competitive advantages to investors in a simple, straightforward way. If a strategic direction is not evident after reading any available investor presentations and conference call transcripts, that may be a red flag about the quality of a company's management team.

Ultimately, a company's competitive advantages should be reflected in its financial results. Companies with strong competitive advantages generally do not have to compete intensely on price to win customers, or if they do compete on price it is because they have the scale or cost advantage to do so and maintain attractive profitability. So companies with strong competitive advantages typically see that reflected in an above-average margin profile relative to their peer group. In particular, gross margin, operating margin, and/or EBITDA margin (earnings before interest, taxes, depreciation and amortization, an important measure of profitability) should be higher than peers. Net income margin can be more volatile and thus more difficult to compare because it can reflect different interest expense burdens due to financing choices or different tax rates which have nothing to do with a company's operations or competitive situation or other non-operating or unusual income or costs.

Profitable growth is usually an important goal of business strategy. Successful strategic execution may result in revenue growth that is higher than the industry average level along with strong profit margins. Sometimes profitability may be sacrificed to generate growth, which can be a good strategy if there is a longer-term vision for using scale to the company's advantage.

The most important job of a corporate management team is to allocate capital to generate good returns for investors. Good allocation of capital is based on a solid strategic vision. Cash may be invested in growing the organization, investing in capital equipment or other long-term investments, or in acquisitions of other businesses. A simple way to measure whether a management team is allocating capital effectively is to compare Return of Assets (ROA) across peer companies. Return on assets is defined as operating profit (or alternatively, EBITDA) / total assets. These figures are easy to find on the company's income statement and balance sheet. If a company has consistently higher returns on assets than peer companies, that is likely evidence that its management team is more effective at allocating capital. Ability to keep earning above average ROA year after year requires a sustainable competitive advantage.

Mergers and acquisitions ("M&A") are an important strategic tool for many companies. M&A can be a powerful driver of value for businesses, or it can destroy value quickly if not done well. M&A, like everything else a company does, should be aligned with a strong overall strategy. A good M&A deal is done at a reasonable valuation, and has a rational purpose such as increasing scale, opening new markets to the company, or offers cost-saving opportunities through consolidation. M&A should not be used for "empire building", that is, growing the business for non-financial reasons, and should not be done at an unreasonably high price. M&A may also involve scaling down a business through divestiture of business lines or assets. Similarly, this type of activity should be judged based on pricing and strategic rationale. Businesses are often sold or spun off to shareholders when the management team believes they deserve a higher valuation than the business as a whole is currently receiving in the market, but are being overlooked by investors because they are part of a larger enterprise. Divestitures may also happen because management believes a line of business is not central to the company's operations, does not align with its strategic goals, or is an unnecessary use of management's time and attention.

Understanding strategy provides important context for making financial projections. Important questions to ask are whether above or below market revenue growth rates and EBITDA or operating margins are sustainable. You may choose to forecast revenue growth higher or lower than the industry average based on the company's competitive position and growth strategy. Similarly, expectations for margin expansion or contraction relative to industry average may depend heavily on an assessment of competitive advantage.

Stock analysts predictably approach strategy with a clear focus on financial results. And at the end of the day, a successful strategy will be reflected in strong financial performance for the benefit of shareholders. Management teams should be viewed as caretakers of the shareholders' investment. Every dollar they spend should come back to the company with an appropriate return relative to the amount of risk that is being taken. That doesn't mean high risk strategies are always bad; higher risk strategies may be a good choice if they have a higher potential payoff, but that decision requires careful analysis.

An important decision you need to make as an investor is whether you trust the management team to take care of your money as if it were their own. This decision should be based on the team's past results, alignment of interests, and articulation of strategic direction. Past results can be seen in the company's historical financial reports. Revenue growth rates, profit margins, and returns on assets that are better than peer companies are strong evidence in favor of a management team. Alignment of interests can be judged through management ownership of stock and compensation that is based on appropriate performance goals. Assessing a strategy requires some judgment. Is it clearly communicated? Does it emphasize the company's strengths? Does it take advantage of market opportunities? And lastly, what are the risks? These kinds of strategic assessments can be hard to quantify but will help you understand your companies and ultimately choose the best stocks to invest in, in conjunction with your financial and valuation analysis.

CHAPTER FIVE

FINANCIAL STATEMENT ANALYSIS

Once you have a good understanding of the business' operations and strategy, you can begin to look at financial trends. Each quarterly and annual report will include three important financial statements: an income statement, a balance sheet, and a statement of cash flows (among other things). Earnings press releases may contain part or all of these statements as well. The income statement (sometimes called statement of operations) includes information on revenues, expenses, and profits during the period. The balance sheet gives a current snapshot of the company's assets, liabilities, and net worth (also called equity). The statement of cash flows summarizes the sources and uses of cash during the reporting period, and is divided into cash from operations, cash used in investing activities, such as capital expenditures for property or equipment and acquisitions, and cash provided by or used in financing activities, which includes borrowing and repayment of debt, issuance of equity, and dividends or share repurchases. In addition to these three main financial statements, the annual report will likely contain numerous other financial disclosures such as financial results detailed by division or geographic region. A more detailed discussion of the three main financial statements follows, using the example of Robert Half International Inc, a prominent publicly traded staffing company (NYSE: RHI).

Income Statement

ROBERT HALF INTERNATIONAL INC. AND SUBSIDIARIES
CONSOLIDATED STATEMENTS OF OPERATIONS
(in thousands, except per share amounts)

	Years Ended December 31,		
	2018	2017	2016
Net service revenues	$5,800,271	$5,266,789	$5,250,399
Direct costs of services, consisting of payroll, payroll taxes, benefit costs and reimbursable expenses	3,390,257	3,102,977	3,089,723
Gross margin	2,410,014	2,163,812	2,160,676
Selling, general and administrative expenses	1,821,089	1,646,532	1,606,217
Amortization of intangible assets	1,705	1,563	1,237
Interest income, net	(4,382)	(1,799)	(888)
Income before income taxes	591,602	517,516	554,110
Provision for income taxes	157,314	226,932	210,721
Net income	$ 434,288	$ 290,584	$ 343,389
Net income per share :			
Basic	$ 3.60	$ 2.34	$ 2.68
Diluted	$ 3.57	$ 2.33	$ 2.67
Shares:			
Basic	120,513	124,152	127,991
Diluted	121,602	124,892	128,766
Cash dividends declared per share	$ 1.12	$ .96	$ .88

The majority of an analyst's time and effort is usually focused on the income statement. Most stocks are valued based on various measures of earnings that are reported on or derived from the income statement. The most important items in an income statement are highlighted below:

Revenue

Revenue is the amount of money a company is paid for its goods or services in a given period. It is the product of the volume of goods or services sold during the period and their respective prices. Healthy companies typically report revenue that is growing over time.

Gross Profit

Gross profit (or gross margin) is defined as revenue minus the cost of goods or services sold, i.e. the direct cost of making the products or services that are sold, before general and administrative expenses. Gross margin can provide some insight into how much value the company adds to the products it sells. It is common to analyze gross margin as a percentage of revenues. A high gross margin percentage relative to those of peer companies is indicative of a company that has a highly differentiated, value-added product or service.

Operating Profit

Operating profit (or operating margin) is what is left over after deducting selling, general, and administrative (SG&A) expenses from gross profit. SG&A expenses are necessary expenses to operate a business, but they are not direct costs of producing whatever it is that the company sells. Think of things like executive salaries or the cost of maintaining a human resources or accounting team. Operating profit is sometimes referred to as EBIT, or earnings before interest and taxes, although a business may have other non-operating expenses in addition to those two. Adding back non-cash expenses depreciation and amortization yields EBITDA, which is a commonly used earnings metric for valuation purposes (these expenses may be found on the income statement, on a supplemental schedule, or if not, on the statement of cash flows). Operating margin is often expressed as a percentage of sales, and that is also a critical measuring stick for a business' profitability relative to that of its peers.

Non-Operating Expenses

Expenses reported below operating profit on the income statement are considered non-operating in nature. The primary non-operating income and expense line times are interest and income taxes, though there may be others. Interest expense is paid to lenders when the company has borrowed money. Income tax expense is paid to local, state, and federal governments as required by law.

Net Income and Earnings Per Share

Net Income is the remaining profit after all income and expenses have been accounted for. This is the profit that is theoretically available to shareholders of the business. Net income can also be measured as a percentage of revenues. When net income is divided by the number of shares outstanding, the result is earnings per share (EPS), typically the most important metric for valuing a stock.

Most companies will report both basic shares outstanding and fully diluted shares outstanding. Fully diluted shares outstanding accounts for stock options that are not technically shares yet, but could be converted to shares at the current price (technically, the dilution calculation also accounts for proceeds expected from the exercise of those options). For valuation purposes, analysts use fully diluted shares to derive EPS.

MARK ETTIMER

Balance Sheet

ROBERT HALF INTERNATIONAL INC. AND SUBSIDIARIES
CONSOLIDATED STATEMENTS OF FINANCIAL POSITION
(in thousands, except share amounts)

	December 31, 2018	December 31, 2017
ASSETS		
Cash and cash equivalents	$ 276,579	$ 294,753
Accounts receivable, less allowances of $27,678 and $33,181	794,446	732,405
Other current assets	402,585	404,711
Total current assets	1,473,610	1,431,869
Goodwill	209,958	210,885
Other intangible assets, net	3,149	4,946
Property and equipment, net	125,176	144,887
Noncurrent deferred income taxes	91,204	74,867
Total assets	$1,903,097	$1,867,454
LIABILITIES		
Accounts payable and accrued expenses	$ 168,031	$ 126,937
Accrued payroll and benefit costs	638,769	612,899
Income taxes payable	12,536	7,877
Current portion of notes payable and other indebtedness	200	183
Total current liabilities	819,536	747,896
Notes payable and other indebtedness, less current portion	457	657
Other liabilities	19,906	13,636
Total liabilities	839,899	762,189
Commitments and Contingencies (Note J)		
STOCKHOLDERS' EQUITY		
Preferred stock, $.001 par value authorized 5,000,000 shares; issued and outstanding zero shares	—	—
Common stock, $.001 par value authorized 260,000,000 shares; issued and outstanding 119,078,491 and 124,261,458 shares	119	124
Capital surplus	1,079,188	1,064,601
Accumulated other comprehensive (loss) income	(16,109)	3,507
Retained earnings	—	37,033
Total stockholders' equity	1,063,198	1,105,265
Total liabilities and stockholders' equity	$1,903,097	$1,867,454

The balance sheet is a snapshot of the company's financial position at the end of the reporting period, and it contains valuable details on a company's financial position. The basic structure of a balance sheet is Assets - Liabilities = Net Worth (also called Stockholders' Equity). Using some basic algebra, that means total assets will always equal the sum of liabilities and stockholders' equity. The

43

balance sheet contains some important information for the equity research analyst.

Current Assets

The current assets category includes cash and assets that can be converted to cash in a short period of time, such as receivables (money owed from customers), inventories (raw materials, partially built products, and products that have not yet been sold), or short term investments. If a company is performing poorly, you may want to start keeping an eye on cash. If cash is running low, the company may need to raise additional money by borrowing or selling more stock. Selling more stock reduces earnings per share and dilutes existing stockholders' ownership stake in a company, and therefore generally reduces the value of a share of stock. This is often a consideration with earlier stage, high growth companies, often in the technology sector, which are not yet generating enough cash to sustain their operations on their own.

Long Term Assets

Long term assets include fixed assets like property and equipment. This category can also contain "intangible assets" like intellectual property (patents, trademarks, etc.). Many companies may also have an intangible asset called goodwill, which is an accounting artifact resulting from business acquisitions.

Current Liabilities

Current liabilities reflect money owed to vendors, employees and others as part of the normal course of business that typically must be paid within a year, and can also include short term debt and long term debt that has aged and is now close to maturity.

Working Capital

Net operating working capital is an important concept that is not explicitly reported on the balance sheet. It is customarily defined as current assets (excluding cash and tax-related assets) minus current liabilities (excluding debt and tax-related liabilities). Working capital gives an idea of how much cash the business needs to fund its daily operations. Businesses that manage working capital efficiently can generate higher returns on invested capital. Growth in working capital needs can suck cash that would otherwise be used for other investments or returned to shareholders, and vice versa.

Long Term Liabilities

The most important long-term liability is usually long-term debt (sometimes referred to as loans, notes, or bonds) which the company uses to fund its operations. Debt can improve shareholders' returns on investment by requiring less equity capital to be invested upfront to generate the same amount of profit, but can also be dangerous. If debt cannot be repaid, the value of the stock can quickly go to zero. The most important part of analyzing a balance sheet for most investors will be determining if a debt load (both short term and long term) is sustainable. Analysts often compare the ratio of debt to EBITDA as a way to compare debt loads across companies. If there is an imminent concern about the debt load, comparing EBITDA to interest expense is a quick way to measure a company's ability to service its debt. The notes to the financial statement will include important information about the company's debt such as interest rate and maturity

Stockholders' Equity

Stockholders' Equity is mathematically equal to the excess value of assets after deducting liabilities. Equity capital raised by the company is reflected here. Stockholders' equity is increased when the company earns net income or decreased when the company generates losses (retained earnings / losses), and is reduced by dividends and share buybacks. It is important to remember that the book value of equity \does not necessarily correlate to the market value of equity. Most of the time, this section of the balance sheet will not require much focus from the analyst.

Statement of Cash Flows

The income statement explains a company's profitability in a given period, but profitability and cash flow are not always the same thing. Because of various concepts incorporated in generally accepted accounting principles, the timing of income may not necessarily match the timing of cash flows. For example, say a company makes an investment in a new piece of equipment needed to operate a business, and that piece of equipment has a useful life of ten years. GAAP requires the company to expense a portion of the cost of the equipment every year for ten years, even though the cash was spent entirely in year one. That company will report cash flow that is low relative to net income in year one, and cash flow that is high relative to net income in years two through ten. Cash is also impacted by financing decisions of the company, like issuing or repaying debt. The statement of cash flows reconciles reported net income to the actual change in cash that a company experienced during a given period.

ROBERT HALF INTERNATIONAL INC. AND SUBSIDIARIES
CONSOLIDATED STATEMENTS OF CASH FLOWS
(in thousands)

	Years Ended December 31,		
	2018	2017	2016
CASH FLOWS FROM OPERATING ACTIVITIES:			
Net income	$434,288	$290,584	$343,389
Adjustments to reconcile net income to net cash provided by operating activities:			
Amortization of intangible assets	1,705	1,563	1,237
Depreciation expense	64,244	63,930	63,078
Stock-based compensation expense—restricted stock and stock units	44,953	42,191	42,699
Excess tax benefits from stock-based compensation	—	—	(1,822)
Deferred income taxes	(15,885)	44,091	(1,868)
Provision for doubtful accounts	11,914	8,022	9,192
Changes in assets and liabilities, net of effects of acquisitions:			
Increase in accounts receivable	(86,217)	(17,039)	(15,888)
Increase in accounts payable, accrued expenses, accrued payroll and benefit costs	89,715	47,832	19,726
Increase (decrease) in income taxes payable, net	28,900	(9,655)	(8,246)
Change in other assets, net of change in other liabilities	(1,295)	(18,528)	(9,416)
Net cash flows provided by operating activities	572,322	452,991	442,081
CASH FLOWS FROM INVESTING ACTIVITIES:			
Payments for acquisitions, net of cash acquired	—	(1,160)	(2,200)
Capital expenditures	(42,484)	(40,753)	(82,956)
Payments to trusts for employee deferred compensation plans	(46,025)	(36,584)	(27,079)
Net cash flows used in investing activities	(88,509)	(78,497)	(112,235)
CASH FLOWS FROM FINANCING ACTIVITIES:			
Repurchases of common stock	(353,509)	(231,724)	(176,031)
Cash dividends paid	(136,423)	(121,000)	(114,164)
Decrease in notes payable and other indebtedness	(183)	(167)	(154)
Excess tax benefits from stock-based compensation	—	—	1,822
Proceeds from exercises of stock options	—	—	223
Net cash flows used in financing activities	(490,115)	(352,891)	(288,304)
Effect of exchange rate changes on cash and cash equivalents	(11,872)	12,949	(5,918)
Net (decrease) increase in cash and cash equivalents	(18,174)	34,552	35,624
Cash and cash equivalents at beginning of period	294,753	260,201	224,577
Cash and cash equivalents at end of period	$276,579	$294,753	$260,201
SUPPLEMENTAL DISCLOSURES OF CASH FLOW INFORMATION:			
Cash paid during the year for:			
Interest	$ 233	$ 278	$ 266
Income taxes, net of refunds	$137,147	$190,954	$219,415
Non-cash items:			
Stock repurchases awaiting settlement	$ 11,359	$ —	$ 14,688

The statement of cash flows can give some insight into the management team's strategic decisions. Looking at the statement of cash flows over time can give you an idea of how the company allocates cash between different investment opportunities. Management may be growing the business by investing in new assets or technology or acquiring new businesses. Alternatively, management may be returning cash to shareholders through share repurchases or dividends. Investment priorities may change over time. A company should only invest cash in assets or acquisitions if the returns on investment are expected to be high. If management does not have attractive investment opportunities, it may start allocating more cash to share repurchases or dividends for shareholders to redeploy as they wish.

Statements of cash flows generally have three major sections: cash from operating activities, cash from investing activities, and cash from financing activities, in that order.

Cash from Operations

The first line item on the statement of cash flows is net income, which is the same number reported on the income statement. Also reflected in the cash from operations section are the impacts from non-cash expenses like depreciation and amortization and cash costs that are not reflected on the income statement, such as payment of deferred taxes. Non-cash expenses must be added back and other cash costs must be deducted from net income to get to cash flow.

The cash from operations section also incorporates the impact of fluctuations in working capital. Growth of working capital is a use of cash, and vice versa. For example, if a company builds inventory during the quarter, that reflects a use of cash that is not reflected on the income statement. If a company builds receivables, that means it is not receiving cash payments for sales in the current period, which will cause cash flow to be lower than net income for this period. Generally, if a current asset account increases, that is a use of cash and vice versa. If a current liability account increases, that is a source of cash and vice versa. The sum of net income, non-cash expenses, other cash costs, and changes in working capital is called cash from operations.

Cash from Investing Activities

Cash from investing activities reflects purchases or sales of long-lived assets that are not reflected on the income statement. Capital expenditures is often the largest category in this section. Also reflected here are acquisitions of businesses and software development costs. The example statement of cash flows from Robert Half above includes a unique line for deposits to trusts for deferred employee compensation plans, which roughly offsets the cash benefit from the use of stock-based compensation in the cash from operations section.

Cash from Financing Activities

Cash from financing activities shows the cash impact from the issuance or repayment of debt, stock issuance or repurchase, dividends, or other inflows or distributions from owners, lenders, or other sources of capital. Some businesses, like REITS, may be very heavily focused on maintaining and growing dividends.

Net Change in Cash

At the bottom of the statement of cash flows, you will typically see the total change in cash for the period, and a reconciliation of beginning and ending cash balances. (There may also be lines at the bottom of the cash flow statement for things like impact of exchange rate on cash.) Ending cash balance will match the cash line on the balance sheet (and beginning cash will match the cash amount from the previous reported balance sheet) There may also be supplemental disclosures of things like cash paid for interest and taxes for informational purposes.

Free Cash Flow

A concept that is commonly analyzed but not explicitly reported is "free cash flow". Free cash flow can be defined differently, but generally refers to the amount of cash that is available to lenders and/or shareholders after the necessary expenditures to operate the business. It is often defined as cash from operations less capital expenditures, though other investing cash flows may need to be incorporated as well. In the case of Robert Half, cash deposited in trusts for deferred employee compensation plans should be included. Cash spent on business acquisitions typically is not included. "Unlevered" free cash flow would add back cash interest payments, as this metric tries to measure the cash flow available to all sources of financing including both lenders and stockholders.

↗↘↗↘↗↘↗↘↗↘↗

No two sets of financial statements are exactly the same. There will be some variation in the particular line items that are included based on the nature of the business. Furthermore, companies may use different formats or conventions for reporting their financial statements, or they may have businesses that require different accounting treatments than the common ones explained above. The notes to the financial statements typically include all the information you will need to interpret the company's financial reporting. The notes can often have more detail than needed for the analyst's purposes, but are worth reading, in whole or in part, because they offer a richness of financial information that is not available simply by looking at the consolidated financial statements.

While some basic metrics like revenue growth and profit margins are important to nearly all companies, the most important financial metrics may vary from company to company. If you have read the earnings press releases, investor presentations, and earnings conference call transcripts, you will have a good idea which items are most important for your company. What financial metrics do the company and its analysts focus on? Does the company give goals, like target revenue growth or operating margin, or something else?

In this disclosure from Robert Half's Form 10-K, the company shows an adjusted revenue growth rate for each division and geographic region. Starting with reported revenue growth, adjustments are made to account for the impact of different number of billing days in the current quarter vs. last year's quarter, as well as the impact of foreign currency fluctuations. This detail may help investors understand what a sustainable growth rate is for the business to make more accurate projections.

Some important financial metrics may be industry-specific, such as users/volumes, reserves, average ticket size, or any number of others. Some may be company-specific, such as organic revenue growth, or division-level revenue or earnings.

	Global	United States	International
Temporary and consultant staffing			
As Reported	8.0 %	5.8%	16.0%
Billing Days Impact	-0.2 %	-0.3%	0.1%
Currency Impact	-0.6 %	—	-2.6%
Intercompany Adjustments	0.7 %	—	3.5%
As Adjusted	7.9 %	5.5%	17.0%
Permanent placement staffing			
As Reported	16.6 %	16.4%	17.0%
Billing Days Impact	-0.2 %	-0.3%	0.3%
Currency Impact	-0.4 %	—	-1.3%
As Adjusted	16.0 %	16.1%	16.0%
Risk consulting and internal audit services			
As Reported	17.3 %	12.0%	42.1%
Billing Days Impact	-0.2 %	-0.2%	0.3%
Currency Impact	-0.4 %	—	-2.0%
Intercompany Adjustments	-3.5 %	—	-21.2%
As Adjusted	13.2 %	11.8%	19.2%

Most companies will be concerned with revenue growth, trends in profit margins, non-operating factors like interest, taxes, and share count. The most important numbers for valuation are typically adjusted earnings before interest, taxes, depreciation, and amortization (EBITDA) and adjusted earnings per share (EPS), though sometimes valuations can be derived from other metrics such as revenue, particularly if the company is not profitable. Look for trends in growth and profitability. Also look at the statement of cash flows to understand how the company uses its cash. How much is used for capital expenditures, acquisitions, share buybacks, dividends, debt repayment, or other distributions? Does the allocation of cash benefit shareholders? A balance sheet should give you an idea of how risky a company's financial position is. The ratio of total debt to EBITDA, often called "leverage", or the ratio of EBITDA to interest expense, often called "coverage" are common metrics to consider and compare across companies.

An important thing to consider is whether GAAP earnings are the best indicator of a company's financial position. GAAP (Generally Accepted Accounting Principles) is the standard set of accounting rules that companies in the United

States follow when calculating their financial statements (non-US companies use a similar, but slightly different standard called International Financial Reporting Standards or IFRS). By rule, all public companies must present financial reports in accordance with GAAP. However, GAAP can have shortfalls, and many companies choose to provide supplemental, non-GAAP financial metrics to help investors understand the company's true financial position. While these should be viewed with a healthy level of skepticism, it can often be appropriate to consider non-GAAP financial results, perhaps because a company has large, non-cash, non-operating expenses, or because of a unique, non-recurring income or expense that is not reflective of a sustainable level of profitability for the company. Sometimes adjustments may not be appropriate, perhaps because a certain amount "non-recurring" costs seem to recur every year, or because an adjustment is out of line with peer company reporting and presents the results in an overly favorable light for some other reason. Adjustments should always be scrutinized for appropriateness and compared to peer financial reporting practices. To the extent a company reports non-GAAP financial metrics, it will always report a reconciliation to GAAP financials. Professional analysts are likely to consider non-GAAP metrics if they believe they offer a better representation of the company's future cash flow generating ability. Take some time to understand what adjustments a company makes to its financial results and why.

In the table below, disclosed in Robert Half's fourth quarter 2018 earnings report filed on Form 8-K, the company details an adjustment made to remove the impact of a non-recurring tax benefit that the company realized during the period due to the Tax Cuts and Jobs Act. Because the tax benefit will not recur in future quarters, it is appropriate to make this adjustment in order to have a better picture of a sustainable level of income for the company.

NET INCOME AND DILUTED NET INCOME PER SHARE RECONCILIATION (UNAUDITED):

| | Quarter Ended December 31, | | | | Year Ended December 31, | | | |
| | 2018 | | 2017 | | 2018 | | 2017 | |
	Net Income	Diluted Net Income Per Share	Net Income	Diluted Net Income Per Share	Net Income	Diluted Net Income Per Share	Net Income	Diluted Net Income Per Share
As Reported	$113,564	$ .95	$ 47,047	$ .38	$434,288	$ 3.57	$290,584	$ 2.33
TCJA Impact (a)	(385)	—	33,737	.27	4,684	.04	33,737	.27
Adjusted Non-GAAP Measure .	$113,179	$ .95	$ 80,784	$ .65	$438,972	$ 3.61	$324,321	$ 2.60

(a) Included in the quarter ended December 31, 2018, was a benefit to the company's provision for income taxes resulting from adjustments related to the true-up of the TCJA estimate booked in the fourth quarter of 2017. Included in the year ended December 31, 2018, were charges to the company's provision for income taxes, resulting from additional guidance related to the TCJA released in 2018, as well as adjustments to the estimated TCJA impact on deferred income tax net assets originally booked in the fourth quarter of 2017. The fourth quarter of 2017 included a one-time, non-cash charge to the company's provision for income taxes, resulting from the TCJA. The charge resulted primarily from a revaluation of the company's estimated deferred income tax net assets as of December 31, 2017.

Looking at a set of financial statements at one point in time without much context can be challenging. It is often helpful to enter financial results into a spreadsheet to visualize trends over time, and make calculations like growth rates and profit margins, as in the example below, which brings together information from filings and earnings press releases and makes helpful calculations of growth rates and profit margins which can be compared over time.

Robert Half International (RHI)

$ in millions	2016	2017	2018
	FY	FY	FY
Revenues			
Temporary and Consultant Staffing	$4,026.8	$4,011.0	$4,330.6
Permanent Placement Staffing	419.3	439.2	512.0
Risk Consulting and Internal Audit Services	804.3	816.5	957.7
Total Revenue	**$5,250.4**	**$5,266.8**	**$5,800.3**
Revenue Growth Rates			
Temporary and Consultant Staffing	N/A	(0.4%)	8.0%
Permanent Placement Staffing	N/A	4.8%	16.6%
Risk Consulting and Internal Audit Services	N/A	1.5%	17.3%
Total Revenue Growth	**N/A**	**0.3%**	**10.1%**
Gross Profit			
Temporary and Consultant Staffing	$1,510.9	$1,493.7	$1,629.7
Permanent Placement Staffing	418.5	438.3	511.1
Risk Consulting and Internal Audit Services	231.2	231.7	269.3
Total Gross Profit	**$2,160.7**	**$2,163.8**	**$2,410.0**
Gross Margin			
Temporary and Consultant Staffing	37.5%	37.2%	37.6%
Permanent Placement Staffing	99.8%	99.8%	99.8%
Risk Consulting and Internal Audit Services	28.8%	28.4%	28.1%
Total Gross Margin	**41.2%**	**41.1%**	**41.6%**
Operating Income			
Temporary and Consultant Staffing	$393.7	$355.7	$404.8
Permanent Placement Staffing	80.0	77.7	90.8
Risk Consulting and Internal Audit Services	80.8	83.9	93.3
Total Operating Income	**$554.5**	**$517.3**	**$588.9**
Operating Margin			
Temporary and Consultant Staffing	9.8%	8.9%	9.4%
Permanent Placement Staffing	19.1%	17.7%	17.7%
Risk Consulting and Internal Audit Services	10.0%	10.3%	9.7%
Total Operating Margin	**10.6%**	**9.8%**	**10.2%**

(continued on next page)

Robert Half International (RHI)

$ in millions	2016 FY	2017 FY	2018 FY
Other Expense/(Income)			
Amortization of Intangible Assets	$1.2	$1.6	$1.7
Interest Income	(0.9)	(1.8)	(4.4)
Total Other Income/Expense	**$0.4**	**($0.2)**	**($2.7)**
Profit Before Tax	$554.1	$517.5	$591.6
Tax Expense	$210.7	$226.9	$157.3
Tax Rate	38.0%	43.9%	26.6%
Net Income	$343.4	$290.6	$434.3
Adjustments	0.0	33.7	4.7
Adjusted Net Income	**$343.4**	**$324.3**	**$439.0**
Diluted Shares Outstanding	128.766	124.892	121.602
EPS	$2.67	$2.33	$3.57
Adjusted EPS	**$2.67**	**$2.60**	**$3.61**
EBITDA			
Net Income	$343.4	$290.6	$434.3
Interest Expense/(Income)	(0.9)	(1.8)	(4.4)
Tax Expense	210.7	226.9	157.3
Depreciation Expense	63.1	63.9	64.2
Amortization of Intangible Assets	1.2	1.6	1.7
EBITDA	**$617.5**	**$581.2**	**$653.2**

To a seasoned analyst, financial statements are more than a set of numbers-they actually tell the story of a business. Once you have spent some time analyzing the financials, you should be able to start synthesizing the numbers into a story. Perhaps the company in question is in a high growth phase, in which margins and cash flows are low or even negative as the business invests in developing new products and customers. Perhaps it is a mature business with low growth and waning profitability. Understanding this connection between reported financials and a business' operations and strategy is the true skill of a professional analyst, and it may take some time covering a company to develop a full understanding.

Once you have a good idea of the story the numbers are telling, you can start to imagine how the story will develop in the future, and projecting financial results that reflect those expectations.

CHAPTER SIX

PROJECTING FINANCIAL RESULTS

U p to this point, you have done a significant amount of work to understand the companies you are covering, but you haven't actually made an investment decision yet. Before that is possible, you need to formulate a view of what financial results are going to look like in the future. Stock prices are based on expectations about future results, they are not reflections of past results or assessments of the quality of a business. A fundamental job of the analyst is to determine if market expectations for a company's performance are too high or too low. If expectations are too low, the company's performance will exceed them and the stock price will rise, and vice versa. Even if financial performance declines over time, if the decline is not as bad as expectations, that can be good news for the stock price.

INVEST LIKE A WALL STREET ANALYST

In order to forecast financial results, professional equity research analysts build a financial model. A financial model is a spreadsheet that projects what the company's financial statements- or at least what key line items in the financial statements- will look like in the future. Earnings estimates can be found online on sites like Yahoo! Finance or your broker's website, but for analysts with the time and inclination, preparing some basic financial projections of your own can help you determine the value of the stocks you are covering.

Financial modeling can be highly complex, but more complex is not necessarily better. A full financial model requires a detailed working knowledge of all three major financial statements, but you don't need an elegant model of all three financial statements to choose stocks- in fact many professional analysts aren't using full three-statement models. A model is a decision tool, not the ultimate goal of your research. The successful analyst is not necessarily the most sophisticated financial modeler, but the one who understands the company and has a good sense for its ability to perform better or worse than expectations. That being said, a detailed model can help reveal some insights about a company if done right.

At a minimum, analysts should develop expectations for future revenues and profits. A simple model could assume a revenue growth rate and expected future profit margin to arrive at an estimate of net income for next year. Divide that estimate by an expected number of fully diluted shares outstanding, and you have EPS, which can be an important metric for valuation. A more complex model might assume a growth rate and operating margin, and then make estimates for non-operating expenses like interest and taxes to arrive at a net income estimate, which can then be divided by the number of fully diluted shares outstanding to yield an EPS estimate for valuation purposes. An even more complex model might then project cash flow items like capital expenditures and working capital needs to arrive at a forecast of cash. For those who are interested, a more detailed explanation of financial modeling techniques with examples is included at the end of this chapter.

Basic familiarity with spreadsheet applications such as Microsoft Excel or Google Sheets is helpful for organizing financial data and performing calculations needed for creating projections. Professional equity research analysts are expert users of this type of software, but even for new users, it can be fairly easy to learn. Numbers can be input using a keyboard. Calculations usually start with an equals sign, "=", followed by numbers and operators ("+" for addition, "-" for subtraction, "*" for multiplication, "/" for division, and "^" to signify an exponent). Numbers can be replaced with references to another cell in the spreadsheet. For example, if you wish to calculate margin in cell A6 by dividing gross profit in cell A5 by revenue in cell A3, you would simply type the following into cell A6:

$$=A5/A3$$

The spreadsheet application will perform the calculation and display it in cell A6. Users can also change number formats, fonts, colors, and other formatting features using intuitive interfaces generally located at the top of the screen. Tools for creating graphs to visualize data are also part of the user interface and are intuitively set up for beginners. Certain "shortcuts", like copying and pasting formulas, can be major time savers. Investing a bit of time in learning how to use a spreadsheet application can be very productive if you are not already familiar.

When making projections about a business, remember that company guidance is your friend. It is important to be skeptical of company guidance, but it is also important to recognize analysts' limitations. Company management is clearly in the best position to forecast results, and they are motivated to give good forecasts to maintain credibility with the market. Giving unattainable forecasts will only result in disappointment when the results are eventually reported. Guidance is usually the best starting point from which an analyst can then apply his or her own insight. Some companies give more detailed guidance than others, and some do not give guidance at all.

Even if a company does issue guidance, the analyst should look at other sources of information for corroborating or contradictory evidence when projecting financials. Historical results and trends are often the best starting point. How have revenues and profits been growing compared to the same quarter in the prior year ("year over year")? Year over year comparisons are important because they naturally account for any seasonality in the business, but be careful to note if the year ago quarter was unusually strong or weak. Applying an average annual growth rate on a very strong year ago quarter could result in an artificially inflated estimate, and vice versa. It is also important to look at trends compared to the immediately previous quarter ("sequential"). If something has changed in the business since last year, for example if cost inflation has caused margins do go down, or if the previous year quarter was unusual for some reason, then simply looking at year over year comparisons will not tell the whole story.

Peer companies may also provide useful information, as well as industry information sources discussed in Chapter 2. Additionally, the analyst's projections should always incorporate good business judgment based on strategic analysis as discussed in Chapter 4. Should this company be expected to grow faster or slower than its industry as a whole or a particular peer? Should profit margins be expected to expand or contract based on the competitive environment? Is the current level of growth and profitability sustainable long term? Once you have formulated estimates for a company, it is always a good practice to sanity check them vs. guidance, other analyst estimates online, historical results, and peer results. If something looks off, take a careful look at your work and decide if something needs to be fixed.

Below is an example of a simple income statement projection for Robert Half International built using a publicly-available spreadsheet application.

Robert Half International (RHI)

$ in millions

	2016 FY	2017 FY	2018 1Q	2018 2Q	2018 3Q	2018 4Q	2018 FY	2019 1Q	2019 2Q	2019 3QE	2019 4QE	2019 FYE	2020E FYE	2021E FYE
Revenues														
Temporary and Consultant Staffing	$4,026.8	$4,011.0	$1,066.3	$1,088.0	$1,083.8	$1,092.5	$4,330.6	$1,084.6	$1,102.7	$1,127.1	$1,136.2	$4,450.7	$4,562.0	$4,653.2
Permanent Placement Staffing	$419.3	$439.2	$121.4	$135.0	$129.7	$125.9	$512.0	131.6	140.9	132.3	128.4	533.1	554.4	571.1
Risk Consulting and Internal Audit Services	$804.3	$816.5	$207.7	$234.0	$252.8	$263.2	$957.7	252.3	272.8	283.1	294.8	1,103.1	1,213.4	1,310.5
Total Revenue	**$5,250.4**	**$5,266.8**	**$1,395.3**	**$1,457.1**	**$1,466.2**	**$1,481.7**	**$5,800.3**	**$1,468.5**	**$1,516.4**	**$1,542.5**	**$1,559.5**	**$6,086.9**	**$6,329.8**	**$6,534.7**
Revenue Growth Rates														
Temporary and Consultant Staffing	N/A	(0.4%)	N/A	N/A	N/A	N/A	8.0%	1.7%	1.4%	4.0%	4.0%	2.8%	2.5%	2.0%
Permanent Placement Staffing	N/A	4.8%	N/A	N/A	N/A	N/A	16.6%	8.4%	4.3%	2.0%	2.0%	4.1%	4.0%	3.0%
Risk Consulting and Internal Audit Services	N/A	1.5%	N/A	N/A	N/A	N/A	17.3%	21.5%	16.6%	12.0%	12.0%	15.2%	10.0%	8.0%
Total Revenue Growth	**N/A**	**0.3%**	**N/A**	**N/A**	**N/A**	**N/A**	**10.1%**	**5.3%**	**4.1%**	**5.2%**	**5.3%**	**4.9%**	**4.0%**	**3.2%**
Gross Profit														
Temporary and Consultant Staffing	$1,510.9	$1,493.7	$396.3	$408.4	$410.1	$414.9	$1,629.7	$412.5	$420.8	$431.7	$436.9	$1,701.9	$1,754.1	$1,789.2
Permanent Placement Staffing	418.5	438.3	121.2	134.9	129.4	125.6	511.1	131.3	140.6	132.0	128.2	532.1	553.3	569.9
Risk Consulting and Internal Audit Services	231.2	231.7	54.9	63.9	71.0	79.5	269.3	63.8	76.1	79.3	89.0	308.2	339.8	366.9
Total Gross Profit	**$2,160.7**	**$2,163.8**	**$572.4**	**$607.1**	**$610.5**	**$620.1**	**$2,410.0**	**$607.6**	**$637.5**	**$643.0**	**$654.1**	**$2,542.2**	**$2,647.2**	**$2,726.0**
Gross Margin														
Temporary and Consultant Staffing	37.5%	37.2%	37.2%	37.5%	37.8%	38.0%	37.6%	38.0%	38.2%	38.3%	38.5%	38.2%	38.5%	38.5%
Permanent Placement Staffing	99.8%	99.8%	99.8%	99.9%	99.8%	99.8%	99.8%	99.8%	99.8%	99.8%	99.8%	99.8%	99.8%	99.8%
Risk Consulting and Internal Audit Services	28.8%	28.4%	26.4%	27.3%	28.1%	30.2%	28.1%	25.3%	27.9%	28.0%	30.2%	27.9%	28.0%	28.0%
Total Gross Margin	**41.2%**	**41.1%**	**41.0%**	**41.7%**	**41.6%**	**41.9%**	**41.6%**	**41.4%**	**42.0%**	**41.7%**	**41.9%**	**41.8%**	**41.8%**	**41.7%**
Operating Income														
Temporary and Consultant Staffing	$393.7	$355.7	$96.7	$103.6	$102.7	$101.8	$404.8	$106.0	$105.2	$109.3	$108.5	$429.1	$440.2	$449.0
Permanent Placement Staffing	80.0	77.7	22.4	27.4	22.9	18.1	90.8	21.6	25.3	23.8	23.1	93.8	98.4	101.4
Risk Consulting and Internal Audit Services	80.8	83.9	15.3	18.5	25.5	34.0	93.3	18.7	28.8	30.0	38.3	115.8	133.5	150.7
Total Operating Income	**$554.5**	**$517.3**	**$134.4**	**$149.5**	**$151.1**	**$153.9**	**$588.9**	**$146.2**	**$159.4**	**$163.2**	**$170.0**	**$638.7**	**$672.1**	**$701.1**
Operating Margin														
Temporary and Consultant Staffing	9.8%	8.9%	9.1%	9.5%	9.5%	9.3%	9.4%	9.8%	9.5%	9.7%	9.6%	9.6%	9.7%	9.7%
Permanent Placement Staffing	19.1%	17.7%	18.4%	20.3%	17.7%	14.4%	17.7%	16.4%	18.0%	18.0%	18.0%	17.6%	17.8%	17.8%
Risk Consulting and Internal Audit Services	10.0%	10.3%	7.4%	7.9%	10.1%	12.9%	9.7%	7.4%	10.6%	10.6%	13.0%	10.5%	11.0%	11.5%
Total Operating Margin	**10.6%**	**9.8%**	**9.6%**	**10.3%**	**10.3%**	**10.4%**	**10.2%**	**10.0%**	**10.5%**	**10.6%**	**10.9%**	**10.5%**	**10.6%**	**10.7%**

Robert Half International (RHI)

$ in millions

	2016 FY	2017 FY	2018 1Q	2018 2Q	2018 3Q	2018 4Q	2018 FY	2019 1Q	2019 2Q	2019 3Q	2019 4QE	2019 FYE	2020E FYE	2021E FYE
Other Expense/(Income)														
Amortization of Intangible Assets	$1.2	$1.6	$0.5	$0.4	$0.4	$0.4	$1.7	$0.3	$0.3	$0.3	$0.3	$1.4	$1.4	$1.4
Interest Income	(0.9)	(1.8)	(0.7)	(1.0)	(1.2)	(1.5)	(4.4)	(1.5)	(1.0)	(1.0)	(1.0)	(4.5)	(4.5)	(4.5)
Total Other Income/Expense	**$0.4**	**($0.2)**	**($0.3)**	**($0.6)**	**($0.8)**	**($1.1)**	**($2.7)**	**($1.2)**	**($0.7)**	**($0.7)**	**($0.7)**	**($3.2)**	**($3.2)**	**($3.2)**
Profit Before Tax	$554.1	$517.5	$134.6	$150.1	$151.9	$155.0	$591.6	$147.4	$160.1	$163.8	$170.6	$641.9	$675.3	$704.3
Tax Expense	$210.7	$226.9	$38.5	$40.8	$36.7	$41.4	$157.3	$37.6	$45.5	$46.7	$48.6	$178.4	$192.5	$200.7
Tax Rate	38.0%	43.9%	28.6%	27.2%	24.1%	26.7%	26.6%	25.5%	28.4%	28.5%	28.5%	27.8%	28.5%	28.5%
Net Income	$343.4	$290.6	$96.2	$109.3	$115.2	$113.6	$434.3	$109.8	$114.6	$117.1	$122.0	$463.5	$482.8	$503.6
Adjustments	0.0	33.7	0.0	0.0	0.0	(0.4)	4.7	0.0	0.0	0.0	0.0	0.0	0.0	0.0
Adjusted Net Income	**$343.4**	**$324.3**	**$96.2**	**$109.3**	**$115.2**	**$113.2**	**$439.0**	**$109.8**	**$114.6**	**$117.1**	**$122.0**	**$463.5**	**$482.8**	**$503.6**
Diluted Shares Outstanding	128.766	124.892	122.887	122.268	121.443	119.851	121.602	117.966	116.988	115.988	115.988	116.733	112.5	108
EPS	$2.67	$2.33	$0.78	$0.89	$0.95	$0.95	$3.57	$0.93	$0.98	$1.01	$1.05	$3.97	$4.29	$4.66
Adjusted EPS	**$2.67**	**$2.60**	**$0.78**	**$0.89**	**$0.95**	**$0.94**	**$3.61**	**$0.93**	**$0.98**	**$1.01**	**$1.05**	**$3.97**	**$4.29**	**$4.66**
EBITDA														
Net Income	$343.4	$290.6	$96.2	$109.3	$115.2	$113.6	$434.3	$109.8	$114.6	$117.1	$122.0	$463.5	$482.8	$503.6
Interest Expense/(Income)	(0.9)	(1.8)	(0.7)	(1.0)	(1.2)	(1.5)	(4.4)	(1.5)	(1.0)	(1.0)	(1.0)	(4.5)	(4.5)	(4.5)
Tax Expense	210.7	226.9	38.5	40.8	36.7	41.4	157.3	37.6	45.5	46.7	48.6	178.4	192.5	200.7
Depreciation Expense	63.1	63.9	16.3	16.2	15.9	15.9	64.2	15.7	16.1	16.0	16.0	63.7	63.7	63.7
Amortization of Intangible Assets	1.2	1.6	0.5	0.4	0.4	0.4	1.7	0.3	0.3	0.3	0.3	1.4	1.4	1.4
EBITDA	$617.5	$581.2	$150.6	$165.7	$167.1	$169.8	$653.2	$161.9	$175.5	$179.2	$186.0	$702.5	$735.9	$764.8

The business is modeled by segment because each segment has unique growth and margin characteristics. This is a typical level of detail that is easily available in company financial reports and allows for a more accurate forecast compared to a projection based only on total revenue. Projections carry two full years beyond the end of the current year, which is a typical timeframe for equity research analysts. Longer term projections are inherently less reliable and are not necessary for many typical stock valuation techniques.

Professional analysts typically use font colors to denote different types of data in a given cell. Blue font indicates assumptions that are input by hand, as opposed to calculated using formulas or historical results which appear in black font. These assumptions are estimates derived from guidance and other information analyzed during our research of the company. Links to other sheets in the model are colored green.

Revenue

Revenue is forecasted based on year over year growth rates. That means the current period equals the year ago period x (1 + assumed growth rate). For example, 3Q19 temporary and consultant staffing revenue above of $1,127.12 is equal to 3Q18 temporary and consultant staffing revenue of $1,083.77 x (1 + 4.00%).

Profit Margins

Gross profit is modeled as a percentage of current period sales. For example, 3Q19 temporary and consultant staffing gross profit of $431.69 is equal to

3Q19 temporary and consultant staffing revenues of $1,127.12 x assumed gross margin of 38.30%. Operating profit is modeled in the same fashion.

Other Expenses

Amortization of intangible assets and interest expense are modeled to continue at their current levels for the next two years. While some more complex methods of estimation are possible, they are not always superior to simply using historical values or averages, especially when results for a particular line item are stable over time or the line item is very small.

Tax expense is the product of pre-tax income and the expected tax rate of 28.50%. In this case, the tax rate is based on guidance from company management. In the absence of guidance, tax rates can be estimated based on historical rates (only look at 2018 and subsequent tax years due to the major change in tax law starting in that year). Taxes can also be calculated directly based on statute, but this calculation is quite complex following the 2018 Tax Cuts and Jobs Act. This law allows for immediate deduction of capital expenditures, but disallows deduction of depreciation and amortization related to investments made in 2018 and later. The law also caps the amount of interest expense that can be deducted at 30% of EBITDA prior to 2022 and 30% of EBIT in 2022 and thereafter. Not all of this information is easily available, even for public companies. Management guidance and the notes to the financial statements should generally provide enough detail to come up with a reasonable estimate of tax rate without going through the process of modeling the tax statute.

Subtracting all other expenses (and adding other income) to operating profit generates net income.

Share Count

Diluted shares outstanding are estimated based on guidance or based on assumptions about share issuances or repurchases. EPS is then calculated as the ratio of net income to diluted shares outstanding

Supplemental Information

Below net income is a reconciliation to EBITDA, which adds back non-operating line items above plus amortization and an estimate of depreciation. Depreciation is simply assumed to be consistent with the amounts from prior quarters. EBITDA is an important figure in valuation analysis, so it is included here even though it is not reported on the income statement.

The model includes a line for adjustments to tie to historical financial reports, though no adjustments are expected for this company in the future. Many adjustments are non-recurring in nature, but some companies may report adjustments every quarter for things like stock-based compensation. If that is the case, the analyst will need to estimate those figures as well based on historical values, company guidance, or other available information.

Periods

For the current year, annual totals represent the sum of the four quarters, except diluted shares outstanding, which is an average of the four quarters. Annual margins and growth rates are calculated based on those respective sums. Beyond the current year, the model is set up to estimate annual results directly.

Balance Sheet and Cash Flow Items

A more complex model could include a projection of a balance sheet and statement of cash flows as well. A cash flow projection might be especially necessary for companies that do not give good guidance on share repurchases, or for a company with a very large debt load or other situations where cash is of heightened importance to the analyst. However, a model could be simpler than a full three statement projection as well and still be useful. Below is a very simple estimate of key balance sheet and cash flow line items:

Balance Sheet and Cash Flow Items	2017 FY	2018 FY	2019 1Q	2019 2Q	2019 3QE	2019 4QE	2019 FYE	2020E FYE	2021E FYE
Cash	$294.8	$276.6	$269.7	$269.4	$269.4	$269.4	$269.4	$269.4	$269.4
Working Capital	397.3	390.2	389.2	401.2	408.1	412.6	412.6	429.1	443.0
% of Revenue	7.5%	6.7%	26.5%	26.5%	26.5%	26.5%	6.8%	6.8%	6.8%
Debt	0.8	0.7	0.6	0.6	0.6	0.6	0.6	0.6	0.6
Net Income	$290.6	$434.3	$109.8	$114.6	$117.1	$122.0	$463.5	$482.8	$503.6
Add-back non-cash expenses	159.8	122.8	24.1	18.8	20.0	20.0	82.9	82.9	82.9
Deduct other cash expenses	(52.5)	(61.9)	(10.4)	(10.7)	(15.0)	(15.0)	(51.1)	(50.0)	(50.0)
Decrease (Increase) in working capital		7.1	1.0	(12.0)	(6.9)	(4.5)	(22.4)	(16.5)	(13.9)
Cash available/needed for investment		$502.2	$124.4	$110.8	$115.2	$122.5	$472.9	$499.2	$522.5
Capital Expenditures	$40.8	$42.5	$12.7	$28.6	$7.7	$7.8	$56.8	$50.6	$52.3
% of Revenues	0.8%	0.7%	0.9%	1.9%	0.5%	0.5%	0.9%	0.8%	0.8%
Dividends	$121.0	$136.4	$37.9	$36.1	$37.1	$37.1	$148.2	$148.5	$149.0
Per Share		$1.12	$0.32	$0.31	$0.32	$0.32	$1.27	$1.32	$1.38
Share Buybacks	$231.7	$353.5	$72.3	$61.3	$70.4	$77.6	$267.9	$300.1	$321.2
Change in cash					$0.0	$0.0	($7.1)	$0.0	$0.0

This simple projection makes the fundamental assumption that cash balance does not change. That assumption is generally consistent with recent history for Robert Half. As a result, all cash generated by the business is projected to be used to finance dividends and share buybacks. This is not necessarily appropriate for all companies, but can be a helpful simplifying assumption for many mature businesses.

Working capital is simply estimated as a percentage of revenue, which is usually projected to be constant. The resulting sequential change in working capital (e.g. 4Q19E - 3Q19E) is incorporated into the cash flow estimate. Recall that increases in working capital have a corresponding negative impact on cash flow and vice versa.

Other cash and non cash expenses from the statement of cash flow are summarized and added back or deducted from cash flow. For simplicity, they are assumed to be roughly unchanged from the two most recent quarters going forward.

Capital expenditures are estimated as a percentage of revenue.

Dividends are expected to grow at a relatively consistent rate, and the remainder of cash is expected to be used to finance share buybacks. By assuming a price at which shares are repurchased (either the current price or the target price), you model the change in shares outstanding for EPS calculations. Some companies may be net issuers of shares. If so, projected share counts should reflect expected share issuance activity. Companies may add back share based compensation to their cash flow and adjusted earnings measures, but eventually shareholders will have to pay for it in the form of a more diluted share count. In the case of Robert Half, share based compensation is roughly offset by contributions to a trust fund for deferred compensation and cash flow is more than sufficient to fund operations, so additional share issuance is ignored.

↗↘↗↘↗↘↗↘↗↘↗

Overall, the model above is roughly in line with management guidance from the most recent quarter. Robert Half's management team gives guidance for one quarter ahead. In this case, revenue is within the guidance range of $1,525 million to $1,590 million, and EPS is within the range of $0.98 to $1.04. The tax rate is set based on management guidance of 28.5%. Results within management guidance ranges, particularly for a time period as close as one quarter ahead, are a good sanity check for results. If you choose to deviate from guidance, have a thoughtful reason why you are doing so, such as a macro trend, competitive change, or some other factor that you believe management is not fully incorporating into its numbers for some reason. You may also look at management's track record with guidance- do they have a history of guiding too low or too high? If so, you may wish to adjust accordingly. Ultimately, the responsibility for making good projections is your own.

CHAPTER SEVEN

VALUATION TECHNIQUES

T he ultimate question the analyst seeks to answer about a stock is what price an investor should pay for it. There are many techniques for estimating a fair price. In general, these techniques combine expectations about future earnings and risk to formulate an estimate of the current fair price of a stock. Valuation is a subject of many graduate-level finance courses, but at a practical level, many methods for estimating the fair price of a stock are quite simple.

Wall Street analysts mostly focus on relative valuation, that is, how the price of a stock compares to those of its peer companies. There are many valuation metrics that can be used for comparison. The most common are price to earnings, or P/E ratio, and enterprise value to EBITDA (earnings before interest, taxes, depreciation, and amortization), or EV/EBITDA ratio. Of course, more than one methodology can and often should be applied to a stock. Changes in the prevailing measure of valuation, in addition to changes in expectations about future financial results, are a key driver of stock price changes, and therefore very important to analyze.

P/E ratio is the most common valuation metric used to value stocks. It is defined as the price of one share of stock divided by net income per diluted share outstanding. Net income is a comprehensive view of the economic value a company creates for its shareholders, so it is very logical to compare that figure to the price you are paying for the stock. P/E ratio can be calculated using historical (last twelve months) or projected earnings. Wall Street analysts most commonly focus on projected earnings, because future profitability is the most important determinant of the value of a stock.

A higher P/E ratio indicates a more expensive stock and a lower P/E ratio indicates a cheaper stock. Ideally, stocks should be purchased at a discount to their fair value, so all else equal, a relatively low P/E ratio may be a good indicator of value. But valuation analysis is usually not that simple. P/E ratios can be affected by a number of things. Higher earnings growth expectations should result in higher P/E ratios. A riskier earnings profile, perhaps because of a more volatile business or higher debt load, should result in a lower P/E ratio. Those factors are important to consider when comparing the P/E ratio of any two companies. But generally speaking, if you believe two comparable businesses have similar growth and risk profiles, a lower P/E ratio could be a good indicator that one stock is trading below its fair value and presents a good buying opportunity.

Despite being the most common valuation metric, the P/E ratio has some drawbacks. First, it is only useful if a company has positive earnings. Not all companies do, including many valuable, high growth companies that are in an earlier stage of their corporate lifecycle. Secondly, earnings can be volatile and may not be the best representation of a company's ability to produce value for shareholders if they are distorted by unusual and/or non-cash income or expenses. Further, GAAP earnings may not be the ideal measure of value created by a company for its shareholders for various reasons. For example, real estate investment trusts (REITs) often use a metric called Funds From Operations rather than Net Income as the basis for their valuation because GAAP depreciation expenses are generally not considered reflective of actual costs of operating those businesses.

EV/EBITDA ratios are different from P/E ratios because they do not directly measure the value of a share of stock. Enterprise value is a measurement of what the entire firm is worth. If you were to buy an entire company free and clear, you would need to pay the entire equity market capitalization (the price of all the shares), pay off all the debt, and buy out any other minority investors. On the other hand, you would immediately get back any cash that was currently on the company's balance sheet. So the formula for calculating enterprise value is: EV = market capitalization of all common and preferred shares + value of debt + minority interests - cash. Market capitalization can be calculated using price and share count data, and value of debt, minority interests, and cash can be found in the company's financial statements (there is an academic argument that market value of debt should be used for EV calculations, but that is usually not very different from book value reported in financial statements for most companies. Practically speaking, nearly all analysts use book value of debt from financial statements in EV calculations). Fortunately for the individual investor, enterprise value is usually calculated and readily available online on financial websites.

EBITDA stands for earnings before interest, taxes, depreciation, and amortization. It is a rough proxy for income that is available to all owners and creditors of the firm. Since enterprise value is a measure of total value available to all owners and creditors of the firm, it is appropriate to compare EV and EBITDA. EV/EBITDA can be helpful to analyze in addition to P/E because EBITDA is usually less volatile than net income, and therefore may be a more reliable basis for valuation. EV/EBITDA also helps compare the valuation of businesses with a very different mix of debt and equity financing more clearly.

Similar to P/E valuation, EV/EBITDA valuation is dependent on a number of factors. Higher growth expectations should result in higher EV/EBITDA multiples and higher risk should result in lower EV/EBITDA multiples. EV/EBITDA multiples must also take into account the impact differing tax and financing structures. If two companies are otherwise identical, the company with the lower tax rate and lower interest expense should have a higher EV/EBITDA multiple. The table below shows an example calculation of ratios for the staffing industry, as well as estimated growth and EBITDA margins for each company to help contextualize the valuation metrics. Maintaining a table like this is a good practice, and something that is done by all professional analysts.

MARK ETTIMER

	Current Share Price	Current Enterprise Value	EPS 2019	2020	2021	EBITDA 2019	2020	2021
Robert Half International	$54.62	$6,310.3	$3.97	$4.29	$4.66	$702.5	$735.9	$764.8
ManpowerGroup	$83.00	$5,792.7	$7.33	$7.57	$7.99	$844.3	$861.0	$890.0
ASGN Incorporated	$61.44	$4,329.6	$3.11	$3.39	$3.68	$447.2	$482.9	$532.6
KForce	$38.08	$894.9	$2.37	$2.58	$2.89	$87.4	$92.8	$100.5
Kelly Services	$24.13	$1,004.4	$1.22	$1.29	$1.35	$127.4	$139.9	$146.8
Resources Connection	$17.01	$537.8	$0.97	$0.99	$1.01	$57.6	$59.8	$60.6

	Revenue Growth 2019E	2020E	2021E	EBITDA Margin 2019E	2020E	2021E	EPS Growth 2019E	2020E	2021E
Robert Half International	4.94%	3.99%	3.24%	11.54%	11.63%	11.70%	10.00%	8.09%	8.64%
ManpowerGroup	-4.50%	1.23%	2.11%	4.02%	4.05%	4.10%	-14.35%	3.25%	5.50%
ASGN Incorporated	14.78%	6.59%	4.53%	11.46%	11.61%	12.25%	4.25%	9.23%	8.54%
KForce	-5.15%	4.35%	5.63%	6.50%	6.61%	6.78%	3.00%	8.70%	12.26%
Kelly Services	0.45%	3.08%	2.42%	2.30%	2.45%	2.51%	110.20%	6.16%	4.64%
Resources Connection	11.34%	1.04%	1.00%	7.91%	8.12%	8.16%	62.30%	2.08%	2.00%
Average	**3.64%**	**3.38%**	**3.15%**	**7.29%**	**7.41%**	**7.58%**	**29.23%**	**6.25%**	**6.93%**
Median	**2.70%**	**3.54%**	**2.83%**	**7.21%**	**7.37%**	**7.47%**	**7.12%**	**7.12%**	**7.02%**

	EV/EBITDA 2019E	2020E	2021E	P/E 2019E	2020E	2021E
Robert Half International	8.98x	8.58x	8.25x	13.76x	12.73x	11.71x
ManpowerGroup	6.86x	6.73x	6.51x	11.32x	10.96x	10.39x
ASGN Incorporated	9.68x	8.97x	8.13x	19.78x	18.11x	16.68x
KForce	10.24x	9.65x	8.90x	16.07x	14.79x	13.17x
Kelly Services	7.88x	7.18x	6.84x	19.79x	18.64x	17.82x
Resources Connection	9.34x	9.00x	8.87x	17.47x	17.11x	16.78x
Average	**8.83x**	**8.35x**	**7.92x**	**16.36x**	**15.39x**	**14.43x**
Median	**9.16x**	**8.77x**	**8.19x**	**16.77x**	**15.95x**	**14.93x**

To estimate the value of a company using a P/E ratio, an analyst must first come up with a projection of earnings for a company and each of its peer companies. The analyst can then use the current stock price of each company to calculate a P/E ratio and figure out the average for the industry. The analyst may also look at historical valuation ratios for the company and its peers to determine if an individual company is trading higher or lower than its own historical levels, or to see if a company historically trades at a premium or discount to its peers. The chart below shows that Robert Half historically trades at an average premium of about 2.5x (that is, its P/E ratio is usually higher than the peer average by 2.5), but the current P/E ratio is right in line with the peer median.

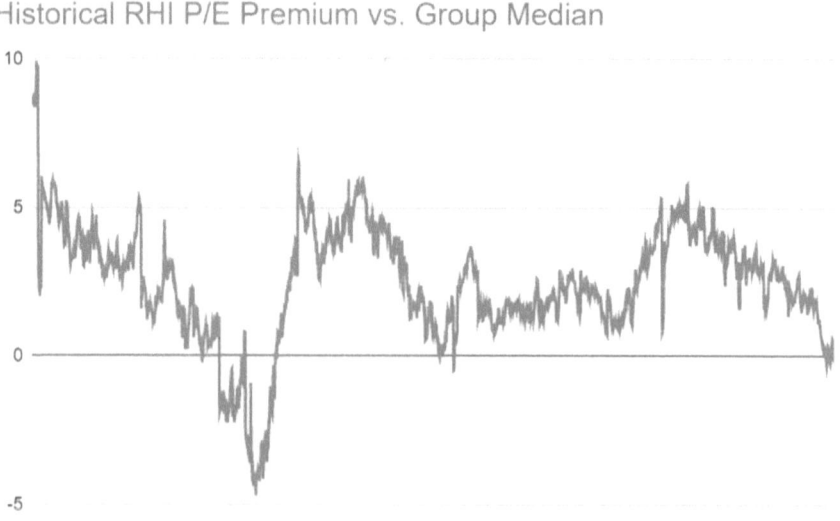

Historical RHI P/E Premium vs. Group Median

Factoring in all sources of information, the analyst will choose a target ratio, and apply that to the earnings estimate to derive the targeted stock price.

An EV/EBITDA valuation follows basically the same steps, but the product of estimated EBITDA and a target EV/EBITDA multiple is enterprise value, not stock price. In order to calculate the target stock price, the analyst must deduct the value of net debt, minority interests, and preferred stock, and add cash to arrive at common equity market capitalization, then divide by the number of diluted shares outstanding to arrive at the target share price.

Some more complex businesses may have multiple business segments that warrant different valuation multiples. Typically if this is the case, operating earnings or EBITDA for each segment will be reported in the notes to the financial statements or in earnings press releases or investor presentations. For companies like these, you may be able to increase the accuracy of your valuation by using a "sum of the parts" analysis. This analysis is similar to any other multiple-based valuation, but each business segment is valued separately using a multiple calculated from an appropriate peer group. Calculate a value for each segment by applying the relevant multiple to that segment's earnings or revenue, and simply add together the valuation of each segment to arrive at the total enterprise value for the company.

The most important principle in relative valuation is consistency. Relative valuation only works if you compare like for like. Estimated earnings can really only be compared across companies if they are calculated for the same time period and using the same adjustments, if any. Differences in adjustments can lead to differences in multiple-based valuations that are otherwise impossible to reconcile. Relative valuations must also be internally consistent. Measures of equity value, like stock price, should only be compared to measures of income available to shareholders (i.e. after interest and taxes have been paid), like net income. Measures of enterprise value should only be compared to earnings metrics before the deduction of interest payments like operating income or EBITDA.

There is no shortage of other relative valuation metrics. For a business with negative profit metrics, for example a fast growing technology company that hasn't reached maturity, analysts often look at the ratio of Enterprise Value to total revenues. For a company with substantial asset value that is easily measured, like a bank, price to book value (i.e., assets less liabilities and preferred equity from the balance sheet divided by diluted shares outstanding) is a common measure. A more value-oriented investor might be interested only in multiples of cash flow (EV to unlevered cash flow or market cap to levered cash flow). When choosing relative valuation metrics, take your cues from what metrics management teams in your sector highlight in earnings releases as measures of value, and, if available, what metrics other analysts are using to value the stocks.

A limitation you may encounter with relative valuation valuation analysis is a lack of appropriate comparable companies. Some niche businesses will have few companies that are truly comparable. One possible solution is to compare to a broader set of businesses that on average have similar growth and risk profiles, but that does not address another limitation of relative valuation, which is right there in the name: relative valuation is relative. If all the comparable companies to which you compare are misvalued, then relative valuation will not yield a meaningful result. Another valuation methodology that addresses these concerns is commonly used by Wall Street analysts as well- discounted cash flow analysis.

The intuition behind discounted cash flow analysis is fairly simple, though the calculation can be more complex. In principle, the value of a stock is all the future cash that will be generated by the company. But in the world of finance, a dollar today is not equal to a dollar tomorrow, which is not equal to a dollar ten years from now. Therefore, estimates of future cash flows must be discounted to reflect their current value (hence the name, "discounted cash flow"). A dollar today is worth more than a dollar in the future because a dollar today can be invested and generate returns during the interim time period. The loss of the ability to use a resource for other purposes is called "opportunity cost". The basic formula for a discounted cash flow is:

$$\text{Value Today} = \text{Cash N years in the Future} / (1 + \text{Opportunity Cost})^N$$

Like relative valuation, discounted cash flow analysis can be used to estimate enterprise value or equity market capitalization depending on which cash flow measure is used, and consistency is critical. Free cash flow after interest payments, also known as levered free cash flow or free cash flow to equity, must be discounted at the opportunity cost of investing in equity, and the result of the analysis is equity market capitalization. Free cash flow before interest payments, also known as unlevered free cash flow or free cash flow to the firm, must be discounted at the weighted average opportunity cost of investing in debt and equity of the firm (referred to as the weighted average cost of capital, or "WACC"), and the result of the analysis is enterprise value. Wall Street analysts more commonly use discounted cash flow analysis to estimate enterprise value because free cash flow to the firm is usually more consistent and does not depend on estimates about future borrowing or repayment of debt.

The opportunity cost of investing in debt of the firm is simple to look up. It is the weighted average interest rate of all debt outstanding. Wall Street analysts use a formula called the capital asset pricing model (CAPM) to estimate the opportunity cost of investing in equity. The intuition behind the capital asset pricing model is the realm of academics and not practitioners, but at a high level, the model attempts to quantify how much exposure a particular stock has to common equity risk factors. Practically speaking, the cost of equity is easy to calculate using easily available input data. The exact formula is:

$$\text{Cost of Equity} = \text{Equity Risk Premium} + \text{Risk Free Rate}$$

Where β is the measure of relative risk, risk free rate is the 10 year treasury rate, and equity risk premium is the difference between expected stock market returns and the risk free rate. Beta and ten year treasury rates can typically be looked up online on financial websites like Yahoo! Finance. Equity risk premiums are estimated by Aswath Damodoran, a finance professor at New York University, on his website: http://pages.stern.nyu.edu/~adamodar/. You can also come up with a simple estimate of equity risk premium by taking an average of historical stock market returns and subtracting the current ten year treasury rate.

An example calculation of Robert Half International's WACC is below:

RHI WACC	
Average Cost of Debt	9.00%
Total Debt	$0.70
Risk Free Rate	1.80%
Beta	1.41
Equity Risk Premium	5.96%
Cost of Equity	10.20%
Market Cap	$6,389.88
Total Capitalization	$6,390.58
% Debt	0.01%
% Equity	99.99%
WACC	10.20%

A discounted cash flow analysis requires estimating cash flows in perpetuity. A simple formula for doing so is:

$$\text{Enterprise Value} = \text{Next Year Estimated Unlevered Free Cash Flow} (\text{WACC} - \text{Expected Growth Rate of Cash Flow})$$

However, this very simple model assumes that growth will be constant in perpetuity. It also requires that expected growth is less than WACC, or the result is a negative number, which is nonsensical. Practically, even for high growth companies, it is impossible to sustain such a high growth rate in perpetuity. If you assume a company can generate 10% annual cash flow growth forever, your forecast will eventually have the company's annual cash flow eclipsing world GDP! However, this limitation is clearly not appropriate in the near term for some companies. Analysts will forecast each year's cash flow until some point in the future when it is safe to assume a steady, mature growth rate that is at or below nominal GDP growth rates, typically around 3 or 4%. A Robert Half DCF analysis is below:

RHI Discounted Cash Flow Analysis				Terminal Value	Terminal Growth Rate
	2019	2020	2021		
EBIT	$333.1	$672.1	$701.1		
Tax Rate	0.3	0.3	0.3		
Tax-Affected EBIT	$238.2	$480.6	$501.3		
+ Depreciation & Amortization	32.0	63.7	63.7		
- Capital Expenditures	15.5	50.6	52.3		
+ Decrease (Increase) in Working Capital	(11.4)	(16.5)	(13.9)		
Unlevered Free Cash Flow	$243.3	$477.2	$498.9	$8,363.3	4.0%
Discount Period	0.25	1	2	2.5	
Discount Factor	1.02	1.1	1.21	1.27	
Present Value	$237.4	$433.0	$410.8	$6,559.8	
Sum of Present Value	7,641.0				
Less Debt	0.7				
Plus Cash	269.4				
Equity Value	7,909.7				
Diluted Shares Outstanding	117.0				
Implied Price	$67.61				

Only future time periods should be included. This analysis is done as of second quarter 2019, therefore only the second half of 2019 and later estimated cash flows are included.

Tax Affected EBIT

EBIT (earnings before interest and taxes, also called operating income) is estimated based on revenue growth and margin assumptions in the financial model in Chapter 6.

Taxes must be deducted from EBIT. Rather than deducting actual estimated taxes which include the benefit of tax-deductible interest, a tax rate is applied to EBIT for estimates of unlevered free cash flow. The resulting value is called "tax affected EBIT".

Non Cash Expenses

Non-cash depreciation and amortization expenses are added back. Other non-cash expenses may be added back for other companies based on the information disclosed in their financial statements. Robert Half has a substantial stock-based compensation program, but contributes an offsetting amount of cash into a trust for deferred employee compensation, so those two lines are excluded for simplicity.

Working Capital

Increases in working capital must be deducted and decreases in working capital must be added back to cash flow. Most growing companies will have increasing working capital, but not all. Working capital can be estimated as a percentage of revenues based on historical averages, and the change can then be calculated based on those estimates.

Capital Expenditures

Capital expenditures must also be deducted to arrive at free cash flow to the firm. Other uses of cash like investments in software may also need to be deducted depending on the company to arrive at free cash flow. Capital expenditures can be estimated as a percentage of revenue based on historical averages and guidance may be given by the company.

INVEST LIKE A WALL STREET ANALYST

Discount Period

The discount period is the number of years in the future that the estimated cash flows are received. The example above uses the mid-year convention- that is, cash flows are assumed to be received evenly throughout the year. Since the first period represents only the last six months of 2019, the discount period is 0.25 years (0.5 years / 2). In 2020, cash flows are expected to be received on average in the middle of that year, which is 0.5 years + (1 year / 2), or 1.0 years, and so on. This is a common assumption used by Wall Street analysts. More simply, you could assume cash flows are received at the end of the year, but this will result in a more conservative estimate of value.

Discount Factor

The discount factor is 1 + the discount rate raised to the power of the discount period. For example, the discount factor in 2021 is $(1+10.20\%)^2$ or 1.21. The projected cash flow is divided by the discount factor to produce the present value of the expected cash flow.

Terminal Value

Terminal value is an estimate of the value of all future cash flows (after 2021 in the example above). To calculate the terminal value, multiply the last period's cash flow by (1 + assumed terminal growth rate), then divide by (WACC - assumed terminal growth rate).

Last period cash flow(1+terminal growth rate)/(WACC - terminal growth rate)

86

The terminal growth rate is usually assumed to be no higher than long-term, nominal GDP growth, about 3-4%. Due to the mechanics of the terminal value calculation, the discount period for the terminal value should be the number of years from the valuation date until the *beginning* of the terminal period. In the example above, that is 6/30/19 to 1/1/2022, or 2.5 years.

An alternative method of calculating terminal value is to use a relative valuation multiple such as EV/EBITDA. Simply take EBITDA in the terminal year and apply a multiple based on current peers or a long-term average to produce a value which can then be discounted to the present as with any other cash flow. This methodology is simple and avoids some of the technical challenges of selecting a discount rate and terminal growth rate, but a poor choice of multiple can result in a valuation that is not useful.

Calculating the Implied Stock Price

Once the present value of each cash flow and the terminal value have been calculated, the present values are summed. If unlevered free cash flows are being discounted, this value is equal to the target enterprise value of the firm. If free cash flows to equity are being discounted, the sum of present values is equal to the target market capitalization. The target stock price can be easily derived from these values by converting enterprise value to market cap if necessary and then dividing by diluted shares outstanding.

↗↘↗↘↗↘↗↘↗↘↗

Analyzing the model itself can also can lead to some useful insights, for example, cash flows further in the future are less valuable than near term cash flows. That is true because of the mathematics of the model, but it also makes intuitive sense. Cash flows further in the future carry a higher opportunity cost than cash today because of the impact of compounding interest; also, estimates further in the future are inherently riskier and harder to rely on.

Discounted cash flow valuations can be very sensitive to assumptions about discount rate and terminal growth rate. An analysis of the sensitivity like the one below can help you to interpret the results. As you can see, discounted cash flow valuation is not an exact science, but works well together with other valuation methodologies to provide a supportable target price.

RHI Target Price at Various WACC and Terminal Growth Rates					
	9.20%	9.70%	10.20%	10.70%	11.20%
3%	$68.49	$63.60	$59.39	$55.73	$52.52
4%	$80.08	$73.32	$67.61	$62.83	$58.67
5%	$97.19	$87.17	$79.08	$72.41	$66.82

Always sanity check the results of your discounted cash flow analysis. If the results are very different from the current market price or other estimates of value, first take that as a sign that you need to double check your assumptions and calculations before jumping to extreme conclusions about valuation. Assuming your model is working correctly, comb the financial statements to see if there are sources or uses of cash that are missing from your analysis, and check your growth and discount rate assumptions to ensure they are reasonable. Always come up with fair value estimates using more than one methodology to provide a more robust basis for your target price.

Once you have come up with a few different estimates of fair value, you can compare and analyze them to choose a target price for the stock. Take into account all the work you have done to this point in selecting a target price. Your choice of target price should be consistent with your research findings about the company and industry and your valuation work. In the case of Robert Half, the valuation analysis is summarized below:

		Multiple	Earning Measure	Net Debt	Equity Value	Shares
Current Price	$54.62					
DCF Implied Price	$67.61					
Peer Average 2019E P/E	$67.05	16.89x	$3.97			
Peer Average 2019E EV/EBITDA	$52.83	8.80x	$702.50	$0.70	$6,180.90	116.988
Peer Average 2020E P/E	$68.34	15.92x	$4.29			
Peer Average 2020E EV/EBITDA	$52.23	8.30x	$735.90	$0.70	$6,110.00	116.988
Peer Average 2021E P/E	$69.79	14.97x	$4.66			
Peer Average 2021E EV/EBITDA	$51.32	7.85x	$764.80	$0.70	$6,003.60	116.988
		Implied 2019 P/E	Implied 2020 P/E	Implied 2021 P/E		
Year End Target Price	**$68.00**	17.13x	15.84x	14.58x		
Implied Upside (Downside)	24.50%					

Various relative and discounted cash flow analyses result in a valuation range between $51 and $70, which is a rather wide range. Compared to the market price of $54.62 at the time of the analysis, it may mean the stock is slightly overvalued or very undervalued. It is not uncommon for different methodologies to yield different results. Analysts must make a judgment about the most appropriate valuation measures for a particular industry and stock. Certain measures may be too volatile, based on too small a sample, or too sensitive to certain assumptions. Think back to your assessment of investment thesis and risks as well. What could cause the stock to trade to the higher or lower end of your valuation range?

In the case of Robert Half, there is a notable difference between the P/E based valuations and the EV/EBITDA based valuations. P/E based valuations result in an average value per share of $68.39 while EV/EBITDA based valuations result in an average value per share of only $52.13. Interestingly, the P/E based valuations are more in line with the DCF implied price of $67.61 while the EV/EBITDA valuations are more in line with the current market price of $54.62.

At this point we are able to put together an investment thesis and price target for Robert Half. Robert Half is a well-managed company that is growing faster and is more profitable than its peers on an EBITDA margin basis. It participates in an industry that is benefiting from both cyclical and secular tailwinds, and should continue growing for the foreseeable future. Robert Half has a pristine balance sheet with virtually no debt, which puts the company in much better financial position than many of its peers. Historically, Robert Half has traded at a premium to its peers on a P/E multiple basis and I would expect it to continue to do so.

Robert Half trades roughly in line with its peers on an EV/EBITDA basis- 8.98x 2019E EBITDA vs. 8.83x average for the peer group. Based on my analysis, I believe Robert Half deserves to trade at a significant premium on an EV/EBITDA basis. EV/EBITDA based valuation does not take into account the impact of interest expenses or taxes. Robert Half's balance sheet has virtually no debt and therefore virtually no interest expense. Accordingly, Robert Half converts EBITDA to net income and cash flow at a much higher rate than many of its more indebted peers, seen in the lower ratio of EBITDA margin to net margin relative to peers in the table below.

	RHI	ASGN	RECN
2019E EBITDA Margin	11.54%	11.46%	7.91%
2019E Net Margin	7.62%	4.21%	4.28%
EBITDA / Net Margin Ratio	1.52	2.72	1.85
2019E EV/EBITDA	8.98x	9.68x	9.34x
2019E P/E	13.76x	19.78x	17.47x

This is likely the reason why the cash-based analysis agrees more with the P/E based valuations than the EV/EBITDA based valuations. The market seems to be valuing Robert Half based on and EV/EBITDA valuation in line with its peers, and as a result, I believe the stock is undervalued. Robert Half has a history, illustrated above, of trading at a significant premium to its peers on a P/E basis. A conservative target price of $68, in line with peer P/E ratios and my own discounted cash flow analysis implies 24.5% upside from the current market price of $54.62. In addition, the expected $0.32 quarterly dividend implies a yield of 2.34%. For all these reasons, I would rate Robert Half a buy at 6/30/19, with a year end price target of $68.

Cyclicality is a major risk to an investment in Robert Half. Based on the industry analysis in Chapter 2, we know that in the event the economy enters a recession, the market for temporary staffing is likely to contract more than the overall economy, and Robert Half's stock would likely perform worse than a broad index of stocks in that scenario. A strong balance sheet is an offset to the risk of cyclicality, because there are no creditors waiting to take over the company if profitability declines. Competition is also a risk in staffing, where competitive intensity is high and customers have many options for staffing services. Notably, the highest growth segment of the business, Risk Consulting and Internal Audit Services, is also the smallest and somewhat less core to RHI's business and may face tougher competition from larger accounting and consulting firms. Further, there is no specific catalyst for Robert Half's prevailing valuation multiple to rise to historical levels. Catalysts, meaning some specific event that is expected to result in realization of the investment thesis, are often important to identify in advance. In this case, the investment thesis depends on the market gradually realizing its error and adjusting its valuation. But as the great economist and investor John Maynard Keynes once said, "the market can stay irrational longer than you can stay solvent". Fortunately, with a blue chip company like Robert Half, long term investors can afford to wait for the market to catch up. Although on balance they do not ruin the case for investing in Robert Half stock, these risks will be important to monitor on a regular basis and could potentially cause a change in recommendation.

This case study of Robert Half is one example of an investment thesis and price target, but every company is different, and therefore every analysis you do will have unique challenges. The investment thesis may be based on an opinion about improving or deteriorating financial performance relative to market expectations, valuation anomalies that are expected to correct over time, or even specific events like potential addition to an index or M&A activity. The possible risks will vary widely as well based on your analysis of the specific industry and company dynamics at play.

Valuation techniques do not spit out exact answers to the complicated question of what a stock is worth. Picking a stock is a little like picking which baseball player you would want on your team and at what salary by comparing the back of his baseball card to some other players at his position. There are a lot of statistics, and each one provides a point of reference, but there is no perfect measure of a player's value, or way to predict what his value will be next year. The ultimate determination of the value of a stock depends on the good judgment of the analyst. Use these techniques along with a dose of common business sense to make a decision about which stocks you want to own.

CHAPTER EIGHT

UPDATE YOUR OUTLOOK

Once you have begun covering a company like a professional equity research analyst, you will want to follow the news every day and keep track of anything that might affect your companies' performance and valuation. Sometimes stocks will be influenced by general news, things like GDP reports, Federal Reserve action on interest rates, or major geopolitical developments. Sometimes news will be specific to your sector, like changes in regulations that affect certain business activities. Keeping track of these developments will help you understand fluctuations in stock prices and update your outlook for your companies.

Companies themselves often make announcements through press releases or SEC Form 8-K filings. Professional analysts will be subscribed to email updates from their companies so they receive the information as soon as it is available. While an individual investor does not need to be concerned with publishing timely research reports in response to news items, it is still important to check on developments with your companies as they can materially alter your views about their earnings potential or valuation. Following the earnings press release, companies will release their full quarterly report on SEC Form 10-Q. Most of the important information is in the press release, but it is worth scanning the 10-Q for additional information and disclosures as well.

Earnings season is a very important time that typically occurs 30-45 days after the end of a calendar quarter, but timing can vary widely for any given company. Earnings release dates will typically be announced in a press release and posted on the investor relations website sometime before they happen. Mark your calendar and remember to check for the company's reports. The company will typically issue an earnings press release (also filed as a Form 8-K with the SEC) and hold a conference call with analysts to discuss results. Many companies also provide supplemental slideshow presentations to help explain financial results.

When a company announces earnings, analysts will read all these disclosures carefully, and compare them to the previous quarter's report and presentation, noting any significant changes. When you do this, ask yourself what has changed and why? While some companies keep an archive of earnings presentations on their investor relations website, not all do, so it is often helpful to download the presentations and save them for yourself. You should also listen to the earnings conference call, or at least read the transcript as soon as it is available.

Earnings announcements are often reported on in the media. These can be interesting sources of information, and it is important to see how results are interpreted in the news. Analysts should be cautious, however, about relying too much on the analysis done by reporters, particularly reporters outside of respected financial publications like the Wall Street Journal or Bloomberg.

Headlines in particular can be misleading, as they often focus on unadjusted financial results that may not be indicative of the company's performance in the quarter. A company may have an excellent quarter, but if they received an unusual tax benefit in the prior year, for example, the headlines may focus on a large drop in profits. Nonetheless, once you have formed your own opinion about a company's financial performance, comparing your interpretation to news reports can be a useful exercise to help understand the market. Such reports may offer a perspective that you had not previously considered.

You should take note of how the stock price responds to earnings releases (or other news events) and try to figure out why. Don't initially assume the market is wrong or that it is overreacting. If a stock is down despite what you thought was an otherwise good earnings report, look again and see if there is another reason why investors might have a more negative view. Focus on the questions analysts are asking on the conference call- they likely reflect questions they have been hearing from the investment community and usually get at the heart of what is influencing the stock price.

Almost all companies provide financial guidance for future quarters or years in their disclosures. Guidance is very helpful for analysts to understand the trajectory of the business. Although guidance isn't always perfect, companies generally try to be as accurate as possible, and they usually have more visibility into their own future results than investors or analysts do. Ask yourself how this quarter's results compared to previous guidance, and if they are meaningfully different, why? If the company gives longer term guidance, how did it change if at all? Perhaps, surprisingly, changes to guidance are often the biggest reason for a large swing in stock price on the day of an earnings release, even more so than the reported financial results themselves.

You may need to update your outlook for a company following an earnings result. But you must be careful, because sometimes it can take several quarters to confirm a trend. On the other hand, don't be afraid to admit when you've been wrong and revise your outlook accordingly. Update your financial model projections and valuation analysis following any earnings release or other material disclosure or news event to reflect your updated view (financial modeling and valuation techniques are discussed in detail in Chapters 6 and 7).

Companies will also periodically make other types of filings, including ownership-related filings and proxy statements. Companies are required to make certain disclosures about ownership of their stock. Ownership by company insiders is detailed on forms 3, 4, and 5. Forms 13D and 13G disclose large owners. 13D forms are particularly notable because they disclose when an investor has taken a large (5% or greater) position in the company, which may have a significant impact on governance or indicate changing sentiment about a stock. A proxy filing, or form DEF-14A, includes important information about management compensation and upcoming shareholder votes. While sell-side equity research analysts do not own shares and therefore do not vote, investors should take the time to understand their options and vote in their best interests. Contentious votes are rare, but may happen for certain controversial stocks or in situations where an activist investor is attempting to force a management change on a company.

Companies make many other types of filings; these should be scanned at a minimum, but many will not contain news that is material to investors. The most material filings in addition to annual and quarterly reports are often filed on form 8-K. Form 8-K is a catch-all filing that can contain information about any type of development at the company. Earnings press releases are often filed on form 8-K, as well as significant news about executive changes, dividends, debt financing, and other things.

Other significant news events could include announcements about mergers & acquisitions, divestitures, dividend or share repurchase policy, strategic changes, or other things. Any of these may change your view of a company or its valuation. Other companies may also be a source of relevant news. Factors that impact customers, suppliers, and competitors could have an impact on the company you are covering as well, so when those companies make announcements or financial reports, consider what that might mean to other companies in their ecosystem. Think about how actions other companies take could affect the outlook for your company. For example, if two suppliers merge, will that impact costs and profit margins for your company?

In addition to earnings releases, news media, particularly financial media such as Barron's, will sometimes publish opinion pieces about companies that can be very influential and often contain some novel perspective. Any time a story like this is written about a company you are covering, it is a good idea to read it and understand it, even if you disagree with the conclusion.

Analysts must also keep an updated view of the industry as a whole. The companies themselves can be good sources of information about the industry through the reports they provide to investors. Also keep up to date with industry data, regulatory trends, and other factors that influence companies operating in your sector as discussed in Chapter 2.

INVEST LIKE A WALL STREET ANALYST

Social media can also be a valuable resource for staying on top of developments in your sector and companies. Use social media to follow companies, people, regulators, industry associations, journalists, and others in your space. For some companies, this can be critical. For example, you would not want to cover Tesla stock without following Elon Musk. He has made material announcements about Tesla stock in 140 characters or less on Twitter!

Staying on top of developments in each stock you cover, and the industry as a whole, is one of the hallmarks of investing like a Wall Street equity research analyst. Analysts on Wall Street are always the first call of major investors who want to learn about a company or discuss how a recent news event impacts a stock. Keeping your view on the bleeding edge of news flow will not only help you make good decisions, it will also help you understand and synthesize the news into your overall understanding of the stock faster, because you will deeply understand the context when that news is announced. You will eventually get a feel for how news events impact the price of a stock, and what news events require a change in your longer term outlook.

CHAPTER NINE

FIND YOUR EDGE

A t this point, we have discussed how to research an industry, initiate coverage of a group of stocks, build a financial model to project earnings, perform common valuation analyses to determine a target price, issue a buy or sell rating, and regularly follow and update your view of a stock. But how does that translate into above market returns for an individual investor?

Investing in the stock market is a competitive game. Opportunities to invest in undervalued stocks vanish quickly as sharp investors scour the market and bid up prices for attractive stocks. If you have read this far, you now have the basic tools you need to evaluate a stock like a professional equity research analyst, but that alone does not necessarily mean you will be able to earn above-market returns on your investments. By tracking your coverage universe closely, you will be in a position to pounce on opportunities as soon as they arise, but consistently outperforming the market requires finding a competitive edge that is hard for other market participants to replicate.

INVEST LIKE A WALL STREET ANALYST

The Efficient Market Hypothesis is a Nobel prize winning economic theory states that all available information is already incorporated into the price of stocks, so consistently finding investment opportunities that yield better than average returns should be nearly impossible. This theory has gained a large following in the academic finance world and has helped fuel the revolution in passive investing. And it is true that on average, actively managed mutual funds do not perform any better than passive investments in stock market indices. In fact, according to a 2019 study by S&P Dow Jones Indices, 85.1% of actively managed large cap funds trailed the S&P 500 index over a 10 year period and 91.6% trailed over a 15 year period. Most of that underperformance is likely due to drag from management fees and expenses. Nonetheless, most market participants and others who follow the stock market long enough will tell you that there are opportunities to beat the market, but most professionals operate with constraints that prevent them from achieving the best possible returns.

Professional equity research analysts do have numerous advantages over individual investors. Many equity research analysts have been covering the same sector for years, and have built a vast store of knowledge about the industry and the companies that participate in it. They have access to informational tools like Bloomberg terminals that are too costly to be practical for virtually any individual investor. And most importantly, they have direct access to company management teams and big institutional investors whose investment decisions can determine the future course of a stock's price. It will be hard for an individual investor to have as good a sense of market expectations for a company's next quarterly EPS than a professional analyst, so trading around earnings announcements may not be your best strategy.

Nonetheless, individual investors have advantages as well. And knowing your competitive strengths and weaknesses can allow you to optimize your investment strategy. If you have worked in the sector you cover, you may have more business knowledge than any purely financial analyst could hope to obtain. You may have networks with people in and around an industry who can help you understand the businesses you cover and what trends are affecting your sector. Beyond these possible advantages, individual investors can operate without many of the constraints that are imposed on professionals. Professional analysts are limited to covering sectors and stocks that are large enough to support enough trading and commission activity to support their business model. Individuals are free to cover any sector and any sized stock. Smaller stocks can present a good opportunity to play in a market that is not as crowded by professional investors. Because of the regulatory and business pressures on equity research, small and medium sized stocks are not as widely covered as they once were. Professional equity research analysts are required to make an investment recommendation for every stock they cover, whether it is buy, sell, or hold. As an individual, you have no such responsibility. If a situation is too risky or hard to understand, you are free to ignore it. You can't "strike out looking" in the stock market. You can pass on as many opportunities as you like.

You can choose a style that works well for you, such as value, momentum, GARP (growth at the right price), or special situations investing. Different investors' skills and personalities lend themselves to different types of analysis. If you are very analytical and quantitative, a value-based approach that emphasizes detailed financial analysis may work better for you. Someone who is more attuned to market expectations and better at spotting trends may lean toward momentum investing. While all investment decisions should be grounded in the same fundamentals, the individual approach each investor takes and the resulting stocks he or she chooses to focus on may be different.

Maybe most importantly, as an individual investor you don't have to worry about being publicly accountable for your choices. It is very difficult for an analyst to admit they made a mistake when their reputation depends on it, even though every analyst does make mistakes. As a result, you can be more nimble in reacting to news than some professionals. You also don't have to worry about making a seemingly riskier call due to worries about reputational risk. Professional analysts may want to avoid making a bold call or wading into a controversial situation because the cost to their career could be high if they are wrong. You can be much nimbler because your only goal is to make money. Individual investors also have time on their side. They are not accountable for performance on a quarterly or monthly basis. You are able to focus on the long term and ignore near-term volatility if necessary to achieve your long-term investment objectives.

You may choose to avoid competition as much as possible by choosing a sector that has little or no research analyst coverage. This can be a good strategy, though there may be some pitfalls to this approach. First, these may be smaller stocks that are inherently more risky. Secondly, it may be hard to find the information you need to cover the sector. And even if you are able to cover such a sector, there are still likely to be professional investors to compete with even if there are no publishing analysts.

There are also some behavioral pitfalls that all investors, but especially individuals, can be susceptible to. Research has shown that humans are hardwired with certain biases and use certain heuristics to make decisions that can lead to bad decision making. Fortunately, by being aware of these issues, investors can control them. Some important examples are:

Confirmation bias

Only considering evidence that supports your existing point of view. Analysts must be open minded, consider all information, and update their view accordingly. All investment decision making should be unbiased and evidence-based.

Overconfidence

Similar to confirmation bias, investors and analysts often overestimate their own abilities. When an investor concludes a stock is a great buying opportunity, there will be a temptation to bet big. It is important to remain disciplined when investing, even if an opportunity looks to good to be true. And if an opportunity does look that good, take some time to second guess yourself. Why are you seeing a huge opportunity where others are not? Is it possible you have made a mistake? Overconfidence can also lead to overtrading, which can be a drag on returns. Very frequent trading is highly unlikely to add value because short term fluctuations in stock prices are inherently unpredictable and trading is costly because of commissions and bid-ask spreads.

Loss Aversion

One of the most common biases investors share is an aversion to losses. Investors will hold onto losers way too long in the hope that the price goes back up to their cost basis. In the meantime, they may be missing opportunities to deploy the money in much more productive ways. Or, in another situation, fear of loss may prevent investors from taking an intelligent risk to begin with. If you are investing in the stock market, you must accept that you will have both winners and losers and be willing to make investment decisions without emotion.

Availability

People often make decisions based on a piece of news they heard recently, or based on an example from their own past that comes to mind. It may seem smart to connect the dots between different events and benefit from experience or from the wisdom of others who have done it before. In reality, it is not wise at all to replace the weight of all available data with an anecdote or two.

↗↘↗↘↗↘↗↘↗↘↗

Avoiding these common investing mistakes is easier said than done, but falling victim to them can quickly eat away at your investment returns. The most important step in overcoming these biases is to take emotion out of the equation. Gather the data and listen to what it tells you.

Finding your edge can be a long process of trial and error. In simple terms, focus on the situations and types of analysis that you are good at. Learning from your mistakes is critical. Every time you sell a stock, whether it is a winner or a loser, do an honest assessment of your work, whether you were right about the investment thesis or valuation, whether you identified all the risks, and whether there was something you did not understand or predict that affected the outcome. Sometimes, the answer will be luck, but more often, if you are honest with yourself, you will see your own strengths and weaknesses as an analyst in the results. Use that information to your advantage!

CHAPTER TEN

HOW TO READ AN EQUITY RESEARCH REPORT

For investors who have access to Wall Street equity research reports through their broker, they can be a very valuable resource, but only if understood and used correctly. In order to do that, you must remember how equity research reports are written and who they are written for.

The first challenge in reading equity research is knowing where to begin. When reading equity research reports about a company that is new to you, starting with the most recent published report is likely not the best strategy. More often than not, the most recent published piece will be an earnings note summarizing a recent quarterly earnings report. These notes usually assume the reader is familiar with the company in question, and can therefore be of limited value to an investor who is looking at the subject company for the first time. Understanding the different types of reports analysts write can help you find the information you need.

Equity research reports can be broken up into a few different categories. Initiating coverage reports are written when an analyst starts covering a new stock, often because of a recent IPO. These reports are generally the longest, often more than 50 pages, and contain lots of background information about the company and its industry. They will typically have a thorough explanation of the investment thesis and risks of investing in this company. They will also normally include a financial model and valuation analysis to support the initial rating and price target. Even if they are slightly dated, initiating coverage reports are often the best place to start when learning about a new company.

After an analyst has published an initiating coverage report, he or she will publish a note after each earnings release, in which they will summarize the earnings news and update their projections accordingly. Earnings notes are typically brief and focus on current topics. The analyst may or may not change the rating following an earnings release. If the rating is changed, the report will typically be longer and contain an explanation for the change. In addition to earnings notes, analysts often publish brief notes to summarize other significant current events, meetings with management, industry conferences, or other news items which may or may not be accompanied by an update to their financial projections. Take note of what trends the analyst is focused on, as this will typically reflect feedback from large investors who can move the price of the stock.

Analysts also occasionally publish industry outlooks or thematic pieces. These are notes that describe the state of an industry and trends affecting the companies involved. These may be updated annually or more often, depending on the frequency of industry data. For example, an analyst covering the staffing industry might publish an industry update on the labor market monthly after the release of the labor report by the Bureau of Labor Statistics. These reports can be very valuable for learning about a new company or industry.

It is relatively unusual for an analyst to upgrade or downgrade a stock mid-quarter. When they do, analysts usually publish longer, thoughtful notes on the trends and reasons for their change of opinion. These can be some of the most interesting research reports available, even if you disagree with the conclusion.

Equity research reports almost always include a buy, sell, or hold rating (or some similar terms) and a price target right on the front page, except in unusual cases where the analyst is restricted, possibly due to conflicts of interest at his or her firm. Changes in ratings and price targets, when they do occur, can cause major movement in the price of a stock. In the case of an IPO, underwriters are prohibited from initiating coverage until 40 days after the stock begins trading (less time for small companies). The publication of initial ratings after the end of this "quiet period" can be a significant mover for the stock. Stock price moves related to analyst recommendations may or may not be temporary. When an analyst issues an upgrade or downgrade, the firm's sales force will typically go to work diligently calling clients to try to drum up trading activity. Often, they will convince some large investors to buy or sell based on the analyst's recommendation. If a note includes a rating change, take note and understand why, and determine if you agree or disagree with the rationale. Even better, if you sense an analyst is on the fence and may change ratings before it happens, that could be a catalyst for the stock price to move up or down.

Although changes to ratings and price targets can cause a stock price to swing, it is important to view them in the context of the equity research business model. Having the most correct ratings and price targets, while it can't hurt, doesn't get an analyst more money or more clients. Overall, equity research recommendations and price targets are not very accurate! Research has shown that buy and sell recommendations are about as good as a coin flip for making investment decisions, and price targets are even worse. Going further, research has shown that equity research recommendations are systematically biased, that is, they tend to be overly positive on the whole, despite the changes that were made by the Global Analyst Research Settlements in 2003. Sell recommendations are surprisingly rare. If an analyst issues a sell rating (or underweight, or other comparable nomenclature), that is something to take careful note of. Hold recommendations are much more common than sell recommendations. Often analysts who are relatively bearish on a stock will issue a hold rating rather than a sell.

Wall Street analysts depend on access to management and the resulting flow of information for their business model to work. The clients of these analysts are professional investors. They are not likely to rely on an analyst's rating or price target without doing their own homework, and don't particularly care how the analyst rates the stock. They do value the analyst's knowledge and access to management. Companies typically use analysts as a conduit for information about a stock. If big institutional investors have a question about a stock, they are likely to call an equity research analyst, who either knows the answer, or has a direct line to the company to get the answer (assuming the answer would not constitute "inside information", or information that could be deemed to be both material to the stock price and not available to the public). Investors also value (and pay via trading commissions for) meetings with company management teams, either one-on-one or at conferences that are arranged by equity research analysts. Not surprisingly, analysts want to maintain good working relationships with companies they cover. Issuing a sell rating on a company's stock can quickly get an analyst shut off from that valuable information flow, so analysts tend to be very gentle with criticism and more highly optimistic than is warranted on average. Although equity research ratings may have a positive bias on average, that does not necessarily apply to every individual research report. Still, it is a factor to consider. While regulators would like to believe that equity research reports are fair and accurate sources of information for all investors, large and small, always remember that the report you are reading was written as a sales tool for a large investment bank.

Then there is the question of a rating actually means. Is a stock rated a buy because the analyst believes it will reach a certain absolute return threshold, because it will perform better than a broad index of stocks, or because it will perform better than its peer stocks? Depending on the firm or even the individual analyst at the firm, the meaning of ratings may not be consistently defined, and that can have major implications for decision making. Generally, and regardless of a firm's stated rating definition, analysts will not assign a buy rating unless they expect the price to go up both in absolute dollars and relative to its peers, but there is some murkiness and subjectivity involved.

Keep these factors in mind when evaluating an equity research report. Never make a decision about a stock based on a research recommendation or price target alone. Use published research reports as another tool to gather more information about a company so you can make an informed decision of your own. Initiating coverage reports, industry reports, and thematic reports can be important sources of background information. Earnings notes and other updates can give you insight into what trends large investors are watching and how they might impact the stock price.

Equity research itself can also be a point of meta-analysis of a company's stock. If a stock is not covered by many analysts, that may indicate that the market for the stock is not as well developed, and investment opportunities arising from pricing inefficiencies may be more likely. Overall ratings can also be an indicator (or counter-indicator) of future price movements. If ratings in aggregate are all changing in one direction, that may be an indicator that positive or negative sentiment is just beginning to build, and the stock's price could start trending up or down. If a stock has had overwhelmingly positive or negative ratings for some time, that may indicate that the sentiment for the stock is too hot or too cold, which could eventually lead to a reversal in trend.

For investors who have access to equity research, it is a resource that should not be ignored; at the same time, it should not be overly relied upon. Equity research reports can be a source of investment ideas, a resource for background information on a company, and a peek into the trends that smart investors are looking at with a particular company. Use them wisely!

CHAPTER ELEVEN

MANAGE YOUR PORTFOLIO

The goal of actively managing investments is to generate "alpha", or returns that are higher than those of a comparable benchmark (benchmark returns are sometimes referred to as "beta"). Common benchmarks for US equities are the S&P 500 Index or the Russell 3000 Index. Choosing individual stocks is one important aspect of portfolio management, but not the only one. Other activities, including sector allocation and management of fees and expenses may go just as far in determining your ability to generate alpha.

Wall Street equity research analysts do not have to worry about portfolio management. They simply make buy, sell, or hold decisions on stocks in their coverage universe and leave sector allocation and other decisions to the equity strategy department. But applying equity research techniques to individual investors would be incomplete without incorporating some portfolio management strategy as well.

When investing in stocks, you make two important decisions. First, how will you allocate money between sectors (or geographies if you are comparing to an international index; we will assume investors are focused only on US stocks going forward), and second, which individual stocks will you choose? The sector weighting of the S&P 500 index as of second quarter 2019 is shown in the graph below:

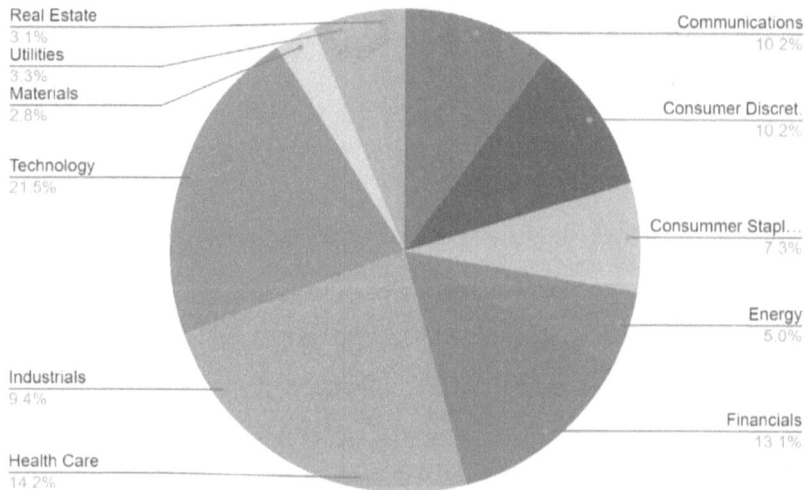

Say an investor allocates 30% of his portfolio to Technology stocks on June 30, 2019 and technology stocks go on to return 20% vs. the overall market, which returns 10%. But the technology stocks the investor chose only returned 18%. The overall return the investor generated is 12.4%. The good news is that 12.4% is 2.4% better than the benchmark! But this investor should realize that he generated positive alpha from sector allocation and negative alpha from stock selection. His performance really should have been 13% if he were an average stock picker. When analyzing your own performance, it is important to compare your stock selection returns to those of the sector you are covering to tell if you are truly generating stock selection alpha. The rest of your over or underperformance is coming from sector allocation. Clearly, investors need to actively manage both their sector exposure and stock selection activities.

In addition to managing sector allocation, investors also need to manage drag on their returns from commissions and other fees. Commissions and fees can come from several different corners. You may be paying fees to an expensive financial advisor. That may be warranted if they are providing important estate planning, tax, or budgeting advice. But as an educated investor, you should be able to closely manage fees you pay for investing advice. Similarly, mutual funds and hedge funds can charge very high fees and incur significant expenses that drag returns. Mutual funds may also charge sales loads, marketing fees, and other fees that can add up to make a major dent in your returns. While there are some benefits to active management, you should not overpay for them. Replacing actively managed funds with a combination of self-managed investments and passive funds can save an extraordinary amount of fees over a lifetime while preserving the opportunity to earn above market returns.

For investments that are self-managed, it is still possible to add up significant costs. Trading commissions are one obvious cost. But even if you have a broker that offers zero trading commissions, trading still comes at a cost. Market makers will charge a "bid-ask spread" to execute your trades. That is, when you buy a stock, you are really paying a middleman slightly more than the seller is receiving. And of course, if you are trading too frequently you are probably not making the best investment decisions. Overly active trading activity can also generate excessive tax payments through realized capital gains taxes that could be deferred with a longer-term investing strategy. Overall, studies have shown that trading costs for individual investors are significant, and the most active individual investors tend to have the worst returns. Another source of costs is drag from cash in a portfolio. Cash can build up if proceeds from sales or dividends are not reinvested. Many brokers offer low interest rates on cash balances. First, try to keep cash invested according to your portfolio strategy, and second, consider interest rates paid on cash balances when choosing a broker.

By acting like a professional Wall Street equity research analyst, you can keep the benefits of active management, strategically manage sector exposure, and keep costs low. First, open an account at a low cost broker that does not charge an account management fee and offers low or no commissions. You may choose to pay a little more in commissions for a broker that offers more services, such as access to sell side research reports, but even that will be cheaper than paying someone else to manage your investments. Since you are actively following stocks in a particular sector, you can choose which stocks you will hold in that sector yourself. You may also choose if you want to be slightly over- or underweight your sector relative to the benchmark. Use sector exchange-traded funds (ETFs) or index funds to maintain balanced exposure to other sectors that is in line with the overall index (but for any strategic over- or under-allocation to your covered sector). ETFs and index funds have minimal fees and expenses, and will allow you to maintain a balanced, diversified portfolio while still benefiting from active stock selection. One of the most popular providers of sector ETFs is State Street, which offers ETFs under its SPDR® brand. A list of sector ETFs and their corresponding ticker symbols are below, but numerous alternatives exist.

Ticker	Sector
XLC	Communication Services
XLY	Consumer Discretionary
XLP	Consumer Staples
XLE	Energy
XLF	Financials
XLV	Health Care
XLI	Industrials
XLB	Materials
XLRE	Real Estate
XLK	Technology
XLU	Utilities

Staffing stocks are a subset of the Industrials sector, so if you are covering staffing stocks, you may choose to invest 9.4% of your portfolio in a mix of stocks from your coverage universe that you have selected and XLI, the industrial sector ETF, to match the benchmark exposure to industrials and maintain diversification. The of your portfolio would then be invested proportionally in sector ETFs according to their weighting in the benchmark index. If you are especially bullish on the staffing sector, you may increase the allocation to industrials and correspondingly cut back investments in other sector ETFs.

It is critically important to maintain discipline and diversification. It can be tempting, especially if you are a person who enjoys taking risk, to make outsized bets on sector allocation or stocks that you have selected. Specify in advance conservative limits on how much you will allow your sector allocations to deviate from the benchmark (for example, plus or minus two percent), or what portion of your portfolio you will invest in a single stock (perhaps three to five percent) and stick to those limits absolutely. Over time, due to relative growth or decline of your stock picks or sector selections, you may start to deviate from your limits without even making a trade. It is helpful to set some parameters on when to rebalance your portfolio. A good rule of thumb might be at least once a year, plus any time a stock or sector exceeds its limit by more than 10%.

Depending on your individual preference, some more advanced strategies may also provide benefits to the individual investor. Long-short pairs trading is one such option. Rather than identifying stocks you think will outperform the market, you simply need to identify one stock that you think will perform better than another for this strategy to work. Taking a "long" position in a stock simply means buying shares and profiting by selling them when they appreciate in value. Taking a "short" position means borrowing shares and selling them. Short investors profit when they buy back shares they have sold at a lower price.

To execute a long-short pairs strategy, you simply buy one stock and sell the other short in equal dollar amounts. Even if both stocks go down, or both go up, as long as your long position performs better than your short position, you will make a profit. This strategy is sector-neutral, so you can invest the balance of your portfolio in a low cost broad index fund, such as a Vanguard S&P 500 Index Fund, and never worry about sector allocation concerns. Before undertaking this strategy, note that unlike traditional long positions, where you cannot lose more money than you invested, short positions have unlimited downside. Your broker can force you to cover (or buy back) your short position if losses grow too large relative to your total portfolio. Not all shares are easily borrowed to execute this strategy. And importantly, there is a (potentially large) cost to borrow shares which means you are starting in a hole with this strategy. Due to these considerations, this strategy may be more appropriate for investors who have much more experience and confidence covering their sector. Another technique that may be especially helpful for income-oriented investors is a covered call strategy. Call options are contracts that give their owner the right (but not the obligation) to purchase shares at a given price called the "strike price". Call options have expiration dates after which the option is no longer valid. If the price of the stock exceeds the option's strike price at expiration, the owner of the option can purchase the shares at the strike price and immediately sell them at the market price, pocketing the difference as profit. If the market price is less than the strike price, the call option will simply expire worthless and unexercised. Because call options have value, investors pay a price for them called a premium.

Investing in options can be very complex and risky, but a covered call strategy adds only limited downside risk to a portfolio if constructed correctly. A covered call is a call option that is sold by an investor for a stock that he currently owns. For example, say you own 100 shares of a stock that is trading at $54 per share. You could sell call options for 100 shares with a strike price of $65. You are paid a premium for the options you sell that you keep no matter what, but you effectively lose the ability to profit from any upside beyond the strike price of $65, where you agreed to sell the shares to the purchaser of the option. If the option expires and the price is still below the strike price, you may then sell more options with an expiration date further in the future.

A few factors affect the premium, or price, of call options. The lower the strike price is, the higher the premium. The further away the expiration date of the option, the more expensive it will be. Prices are also impacted by interest rates and the volatility of the underlying stock. More volatile stocks have higher priced options. When choosing which option to sell, you must balance the income from the premium with the potential loss of upside. The goal is not to execute the options. Choose a strike price that is sufficiently higher than the current price and a term that is reasonably near so that the likelihood of execution is fairly low. But there will not be a market for options that have no reasonable chance of having value at expiration, so choosing which option to sell, if any, is a balancing act.

Covered call writing is essentially giving away potential upside for income today. This strategy can help increase your profits if you think a stock has limited upside. You will find that not all stocks have sufficiently liquid options markets for this kind of strategy to work. Typically only the largest and most actively traded names will have a deep enough options market to execute this strategy. And while executing a covered call strategy is simple, pricing an option accurately is very complex. Your broker may offer online tools to help price options, which can help you decide if a covered call trade is a good value.

If every stock you pick is a home run, then maybe you don't need to think carefully about portfolio management. But for the rest of us, portfolio management is the process of turning our investment ideas into above market investment returns. Good portfolio management requires planning, discipline, and efficiency. Avoiding unnecessary fees and expenses is important, as is managing risk within reasonable parameters. Decide in advance on a maximum percentage of your portfolio that you will invest in a single stock, and the maximum deviation you will allow from benchmark sector weightings. Your portfolio itself is a business, and you are the CEO. You should review its performance regularly to ensure you are managing within your guidelines and minimizing expenses. Drive out expenses, and drive out behaviors like overtrading or biased decision making that drag your returns. Ensure you have a well balanced, diversified portfolio that will generate adequate rewards for the risk you are taking.

APPENDIX: HOW TO PREPARE FOR A CAREER IN EQUITY RESEARCH

Equity research can be a very interesting and rewarding job. For those of us who enjoy the stock market, it can be a fun job. Equity research analysts are at the heart of an industry, and they get to interact with senior executives and sophisticated investors on a daily basis. Despite some headwinds from regulation and trends in passive investing, there is always likely to be a place for equity research analysts, and the career path can be financially rewarding as well.

On the other hand, equity research can also be challenging. It can be intellectually challenging to understand an industry and the companies in it, and constantly keep up with changes in the market. You have to withstand careful scrutiny of your work by sharp investors who won't hesitate to pick up the phone and grill you if they see something in a report that doesn't look right- some even seem to enjoy proving analysts wrong! Because so much is at stake, simple mistakes can have disastrous consequences. And importantly, equity research is hard work with long hours. Analysts are always on call because major news can break that impacts a stock you cover at any time, and you have to be prepared to get to the office, write it up, and speak to clients about it. For these reasons, Wall Street firms are extremely selective about who they hire to work in equity research.

Common academic qualifications for a job in equity research are an undergraduate business degree or MBA, and the Chartered Financial Analyst (CFA) designation. MBA job candidates will be expected to have relevant real world experience, because they will be asked to start at a more senior level with greater responsibility. Whether or not your academic background is in business or economics, your resume should include some coursework or other activities that demonstrate some interest or experience, such as membership in a stock picking club or completion of an extracurricular financial modeling course.

Most equity research interviews are granted through on campus recruiting programs at undergraduate business or economics and MBA programs. Most full time job offers are made following the completion of a summer internship, so recruiting for equity research jobs starts early in your academic career. The best way to get an interview in equity research is to attend a highly regarded business school, but it is not the only way. Some equity research specialties, like biotech, may prefer someone with a technical background like an MD or PhD in addition to a business background. It is less common, but sometimes people are hired after working directly in the industry they will cover as analysts.

If attending a business school where Wall Street firms recruit on campus is not an option, you will have to do some networking to secure an interview. Excellent grades and activities that demonstrate interest in investing are a must for students at any school, but it is highly unlikely that you will get an interview from submitting a resume online alone, no matter how qualified you are. Some kind of personal connection dramatically increases the odds of attracting attention from recruiting departments. Senior research analysts usually have a lot of freedom to make decisions about their team, so networking directly with them is usually the best way to obtain an interview. If you are a student, the best way to network is usually with alumni of your school. If your school has a finance club or investment club, that may be a good starting point for finding alumni in the industry. Personal networks like family friends are also an option for some. Linkedin can be a great tool for finding connections. No matter how tenuous the connection, try to capitalize on any opportunity to make an introduction with an analyst.

If you are ever able to get your hands on an equity research report, they all have the publishing analyst's email address right there on the front page! A cold email or Linkedin message is never as good as an introduction, but if it is your only option, it is better than nothing. Simply be polite, attach a resume, and ask if they are willing to do a quick phone call to explain their job to an aspiring analyst, and do not pester them if you don't get a response.

If you are able to get an introduction to an equity research analyst, see if you can schedule an informal chat to learn about their job, and try to tactfully parlay that into an interview opportunity. And any time you have a conversation with someone in equity research, end by asking if there is someone else you should talk to.

When networking, you should be persistent, but not annoying. A job candidate is probably not at the top of any analyst's to-do list. They may become swamped with work and forget to return an email. A polite note after some time has passed is appropriate. Ask for advice and guidance rather than just begging for an interview. Frequent emails or phone calls will likely get you blacklisted.

When applying for jobs in equity research, one of the most important things you can do is demonstrate a passion for investing in stocks. The job will wear on you very quickly if you are not excited about coming to work every day to cover stocks. Reading this book is a good start! If you are going to apply for a job in equity research, you should be prepared to demonstrate that you follow the stock market closely and invest on your own, or if you can't, at least follow stocks and have well-thought out opinions on them. If you interview for an equity research job, you will almost certainly be asked to present a stock idea. You should not only demonstrate that you have a good investment idea, but also that you have the ability to communicate the idea persuasively. Understand the investment thesis, risks, and have a good estimate of the fair value of the stock that you can talk about in an interview. Some analysts may ask you for both a long and short stock idea.

Related to that, candidates must understand what they are getting into with equity research. It is a difficult job, and no one wants to hire someone and invest time and money in training them only to see them quit after a few months because they don't enjoy or can't handle the work. The hours will be long, especially during earnings season, the time of the year when companies are announcing their quarterly financial results. The travel requirements are demanding, especially as you move up the ranks, as you must go on the road to facilitate management meetings with investors or market your firm to potential clients. If a company announces a large acquisition on Friday, be prepared to work all weekend to analyze the deal and update your view of the stock by the time the market opens on Monday. No vacation is sacred in equity research. You are always on call! A good candidate should be able to subtly communicate that they understand the requirements of the job during an interview.

More so than any other position in finance, equity research requires strong writing skills. Your day to day job will include the production of written research reports that are clear, informative, and persuasive. As a junior analyst, you will need to be able to match the writing style of the senior analyst that you work for. It is important that you are able to write with one voice consistently across all your work. The best way to develop writing skills is to read business publications every day. Business publications like Bloomberg Businessweek or the Wall Street Journal are good resources because they have straightforward, factual styles that translate well to an equity research setting. You will not be asked to write the next great novel! Flowery language is generally a negative, though some analysts do like to inject a bit of personal style into their work. Write simply, clearly, and persuasively. If you did not learn grammar in high school, learn it now! Nothing stands out quicker in equity research than poor writing skills. Most equity research interviews will require that you submit a writing sample. A written report for a business class that you are proud of is a good option.

A lot of people have an image of equity research analysts as hermits who sit at dimly lit desks poring over thousands of pages of financial reports and building spreadsheets in silence. In reality, they are anything but! Equity research analysts, especially as they move up the ranks, spend most of their time talking to clients or company management teams. Equity research analysts tend to get exposure to executive management teams (CEOs, CFOs and other executives) at a relatively early stage in their careers, and it is important to be able to communicate with them on their level. You may be asked to speak publicly at conferences or other events. And you will spend hours each day on the phone with clients answering questions about the companies you cover. You need to be a very strong communicator with good people skills. And remember that at the end of the day, equity research is a sales role. Analysts are employed to convince investors to do trades that result in commissions for their firm's trading desk. Analysts should be great relationship builders, so clients think of them first when they have a question about a stock in their sector. Your ability to communicate and confidence in yourself will come across in the way you carry yourself in an interview. You should be prepared to tell a thoughtful and persuasive story about why you want to be an equity research analyst, and what preparation you have done that will make you a good analyst. Your presentation in the interview should come across as confident and polished, but not scripted, just as if you were speaking to an important client about a stock that you know well.

In an interview setting, remember what skills make a good analyst: attention to detail, written and spoken communication, and analytical abilities among others. Most interviewers ask about strengths and weaknesses. Be honest, but tailor your answers for the job you are seeking. Don't say your weakness is something core to the job of equity research like communication or public speaking. You will be rejected immediately!

Most equity research interviews will also include some kind of modeling test in which candidates will be given a model template and asked to fill it in with working formulas. It may be conducted in a room in the analyst's office with a strict time limit, or it may be given to you to complete at home. If you are not experienced in financial modeling, there are many courses available online in and in classrooms that can help build your skills. Financial modeling is a critical job function especially for entry level equity research analysts. Ensure you have a solid working knowledge of the three major financial statements. In addition to your modeling test, you may be asked technical questions in the interview about accounting topics.

Just as markets for stocks are efficient, the labor market is efficient too. If you are smart, motivated, and well-suited for equity research, you should be able to overcome intense competition for the job with persistence, skill, and tact.

www.ingramcontent.com/pod-product-compliance
Lightning Source LLC
Chambersburg PA
CBHW021420210526
45463CB00001B/462